This Book Belongs To:

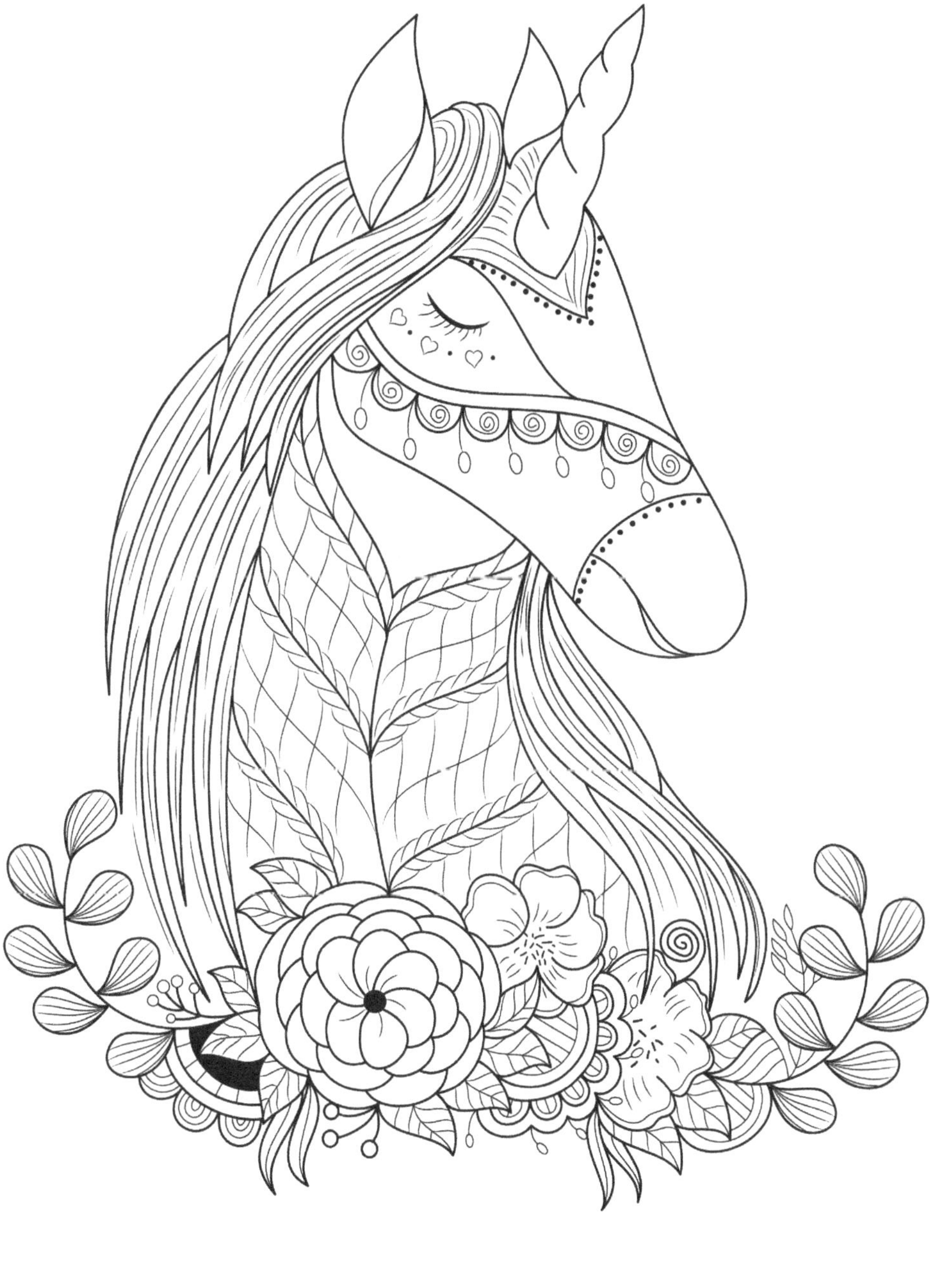

_____

Preview of Coloring Pages

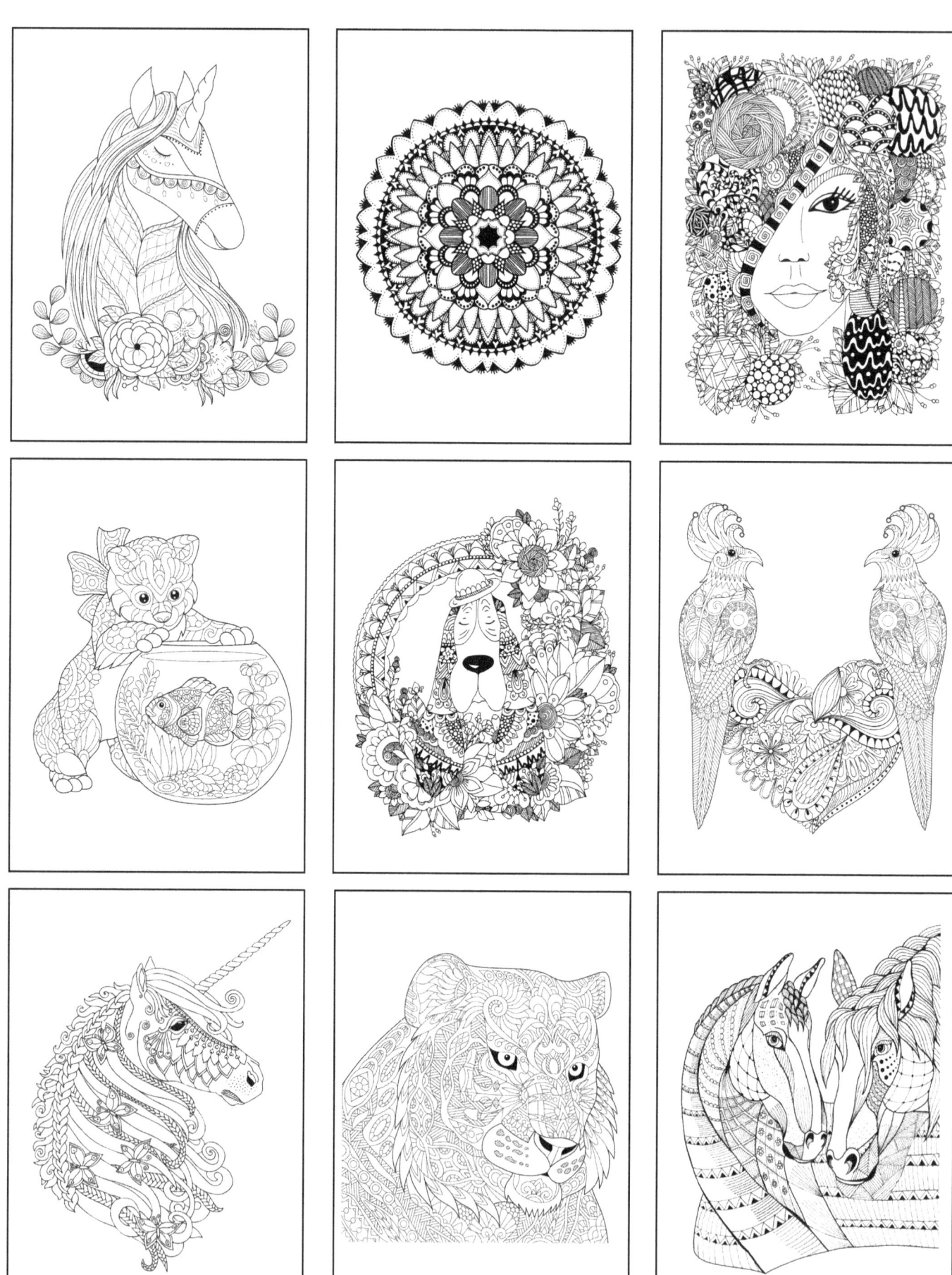

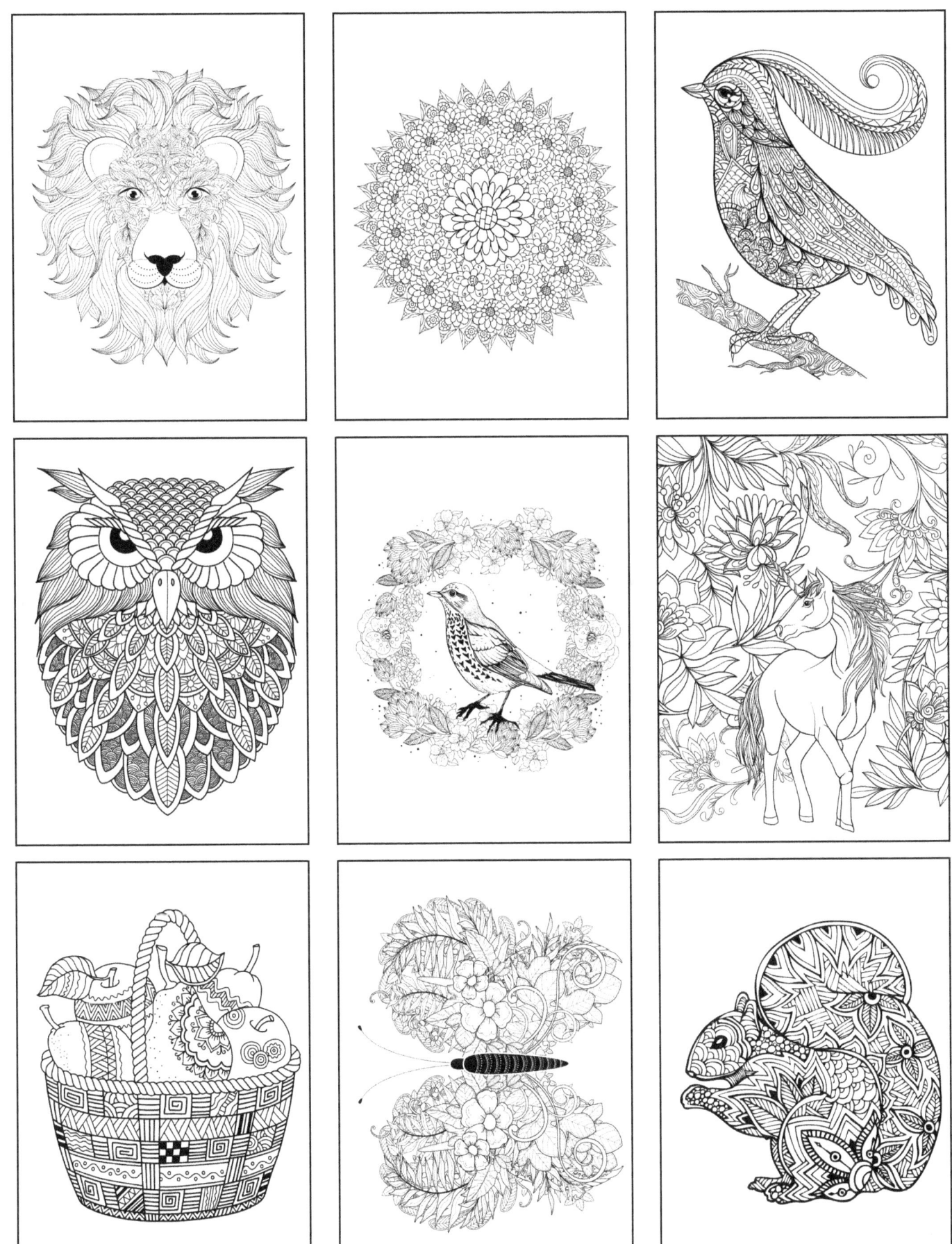

Preview of Coloring Pages

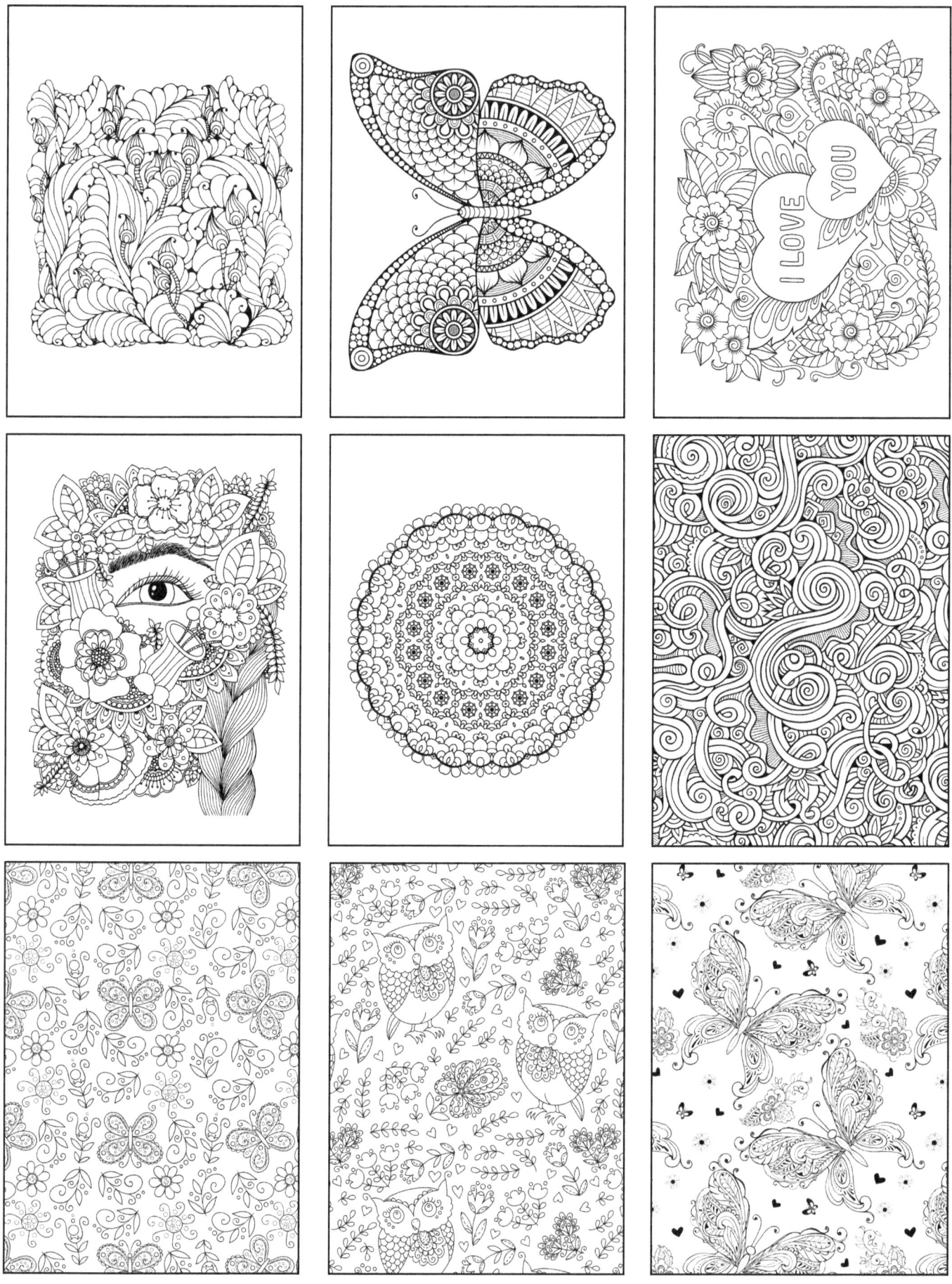

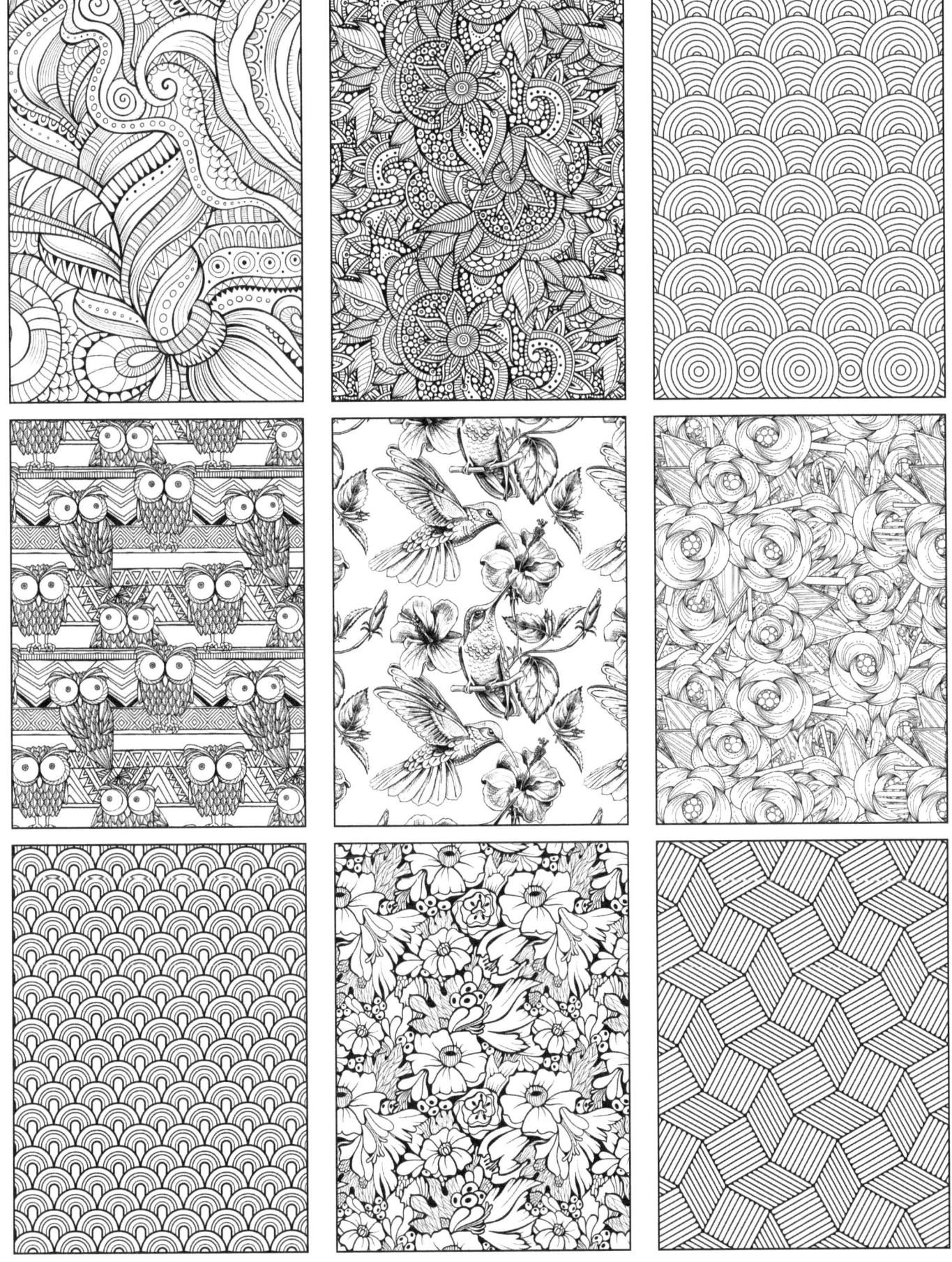

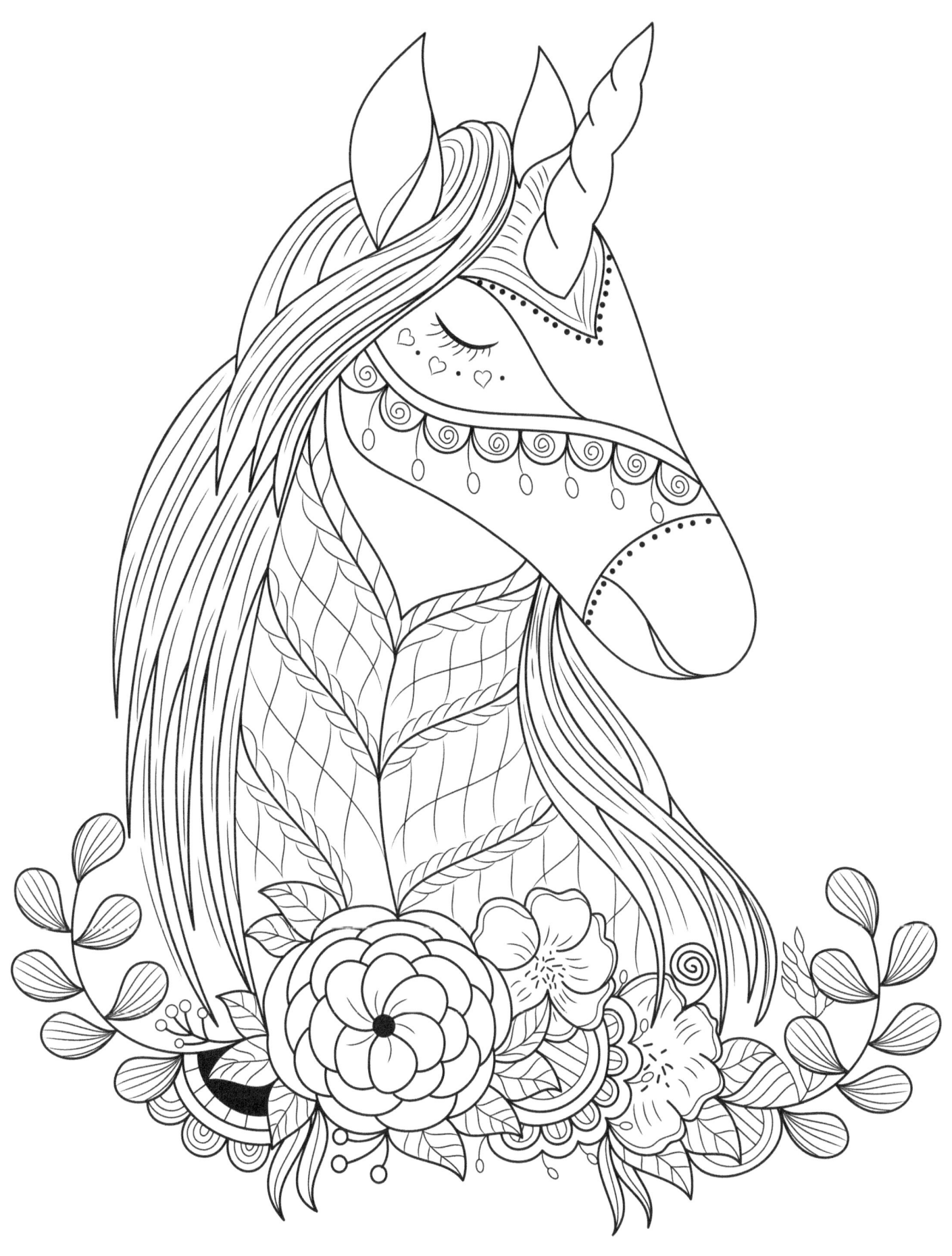

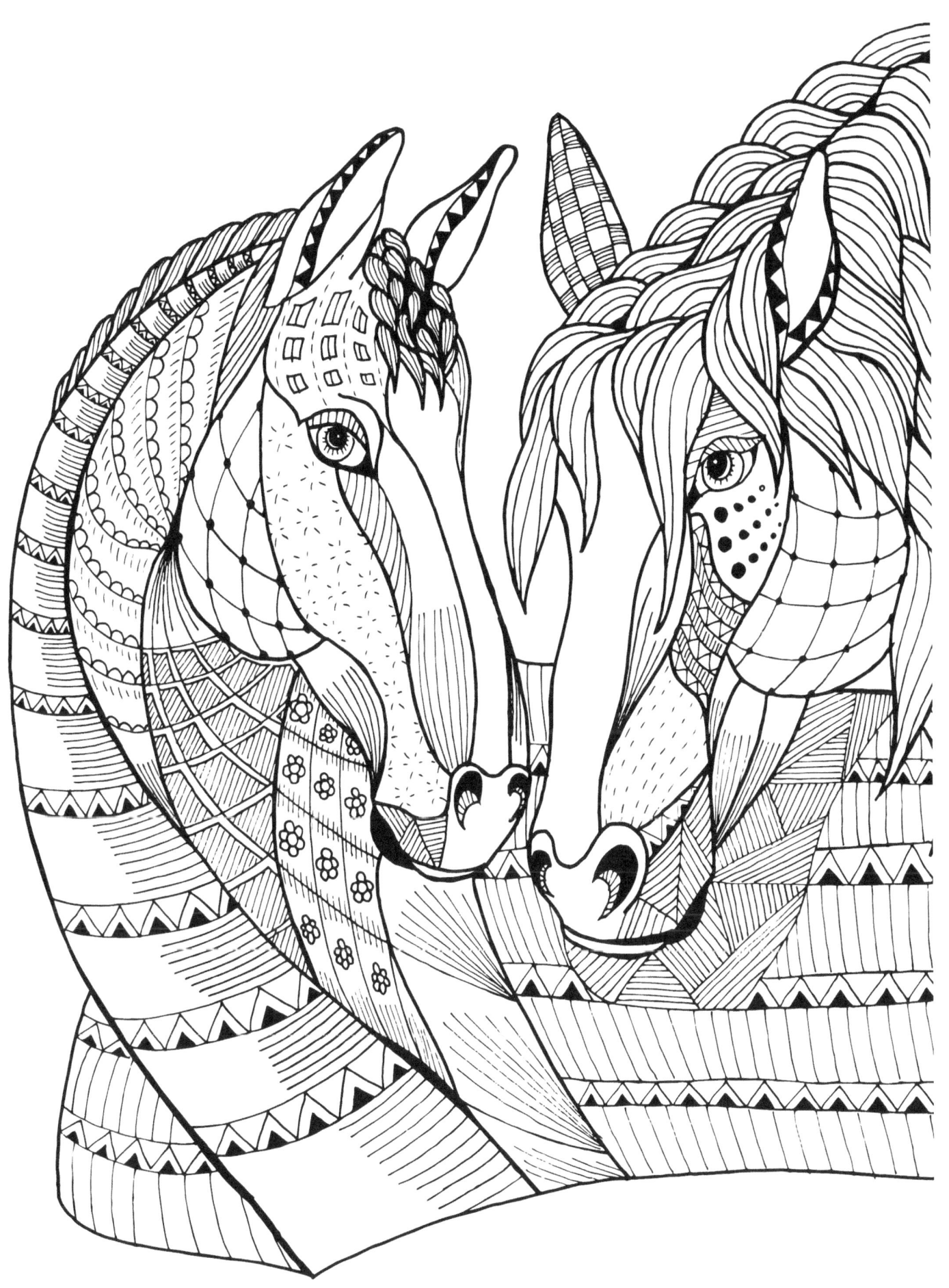

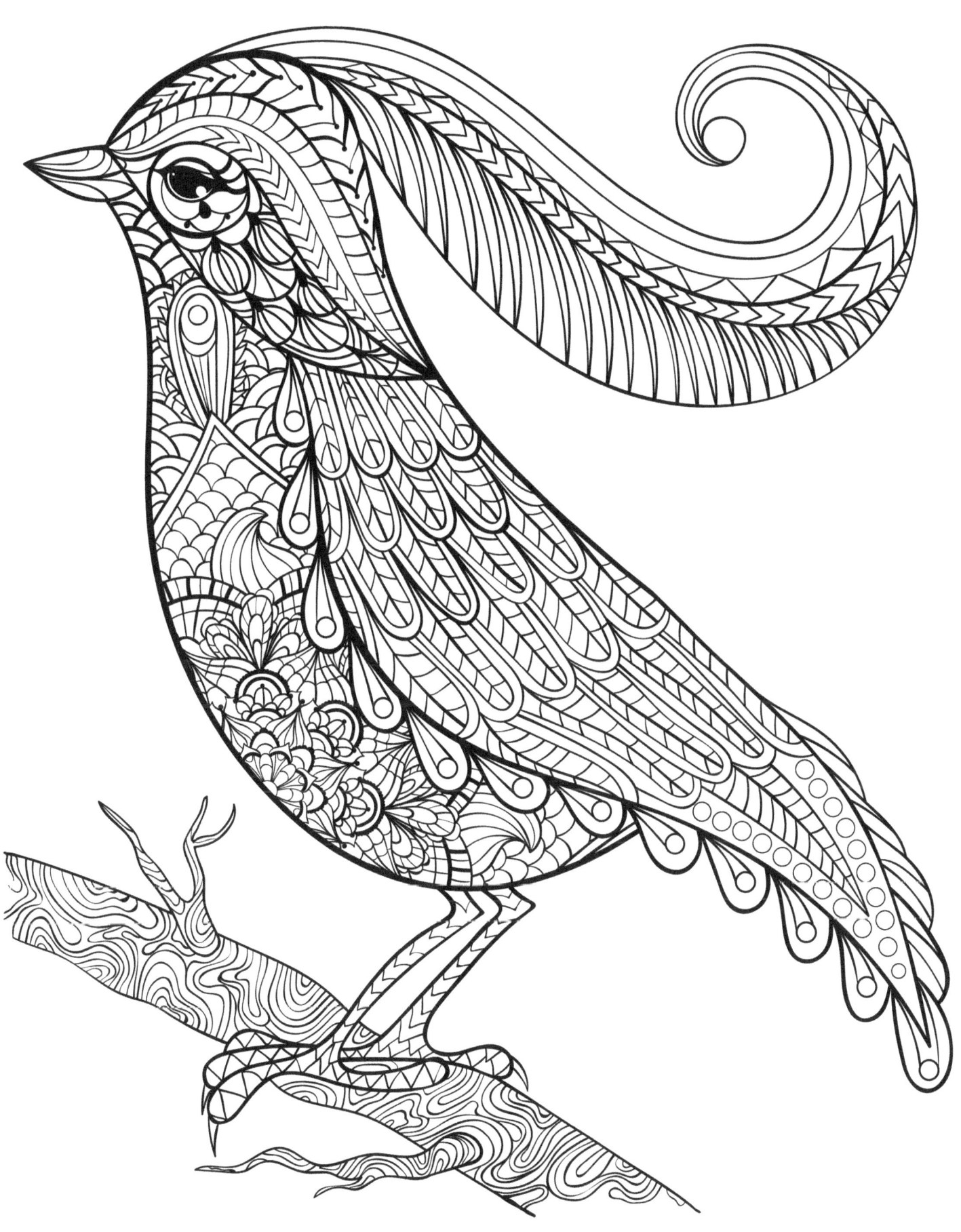

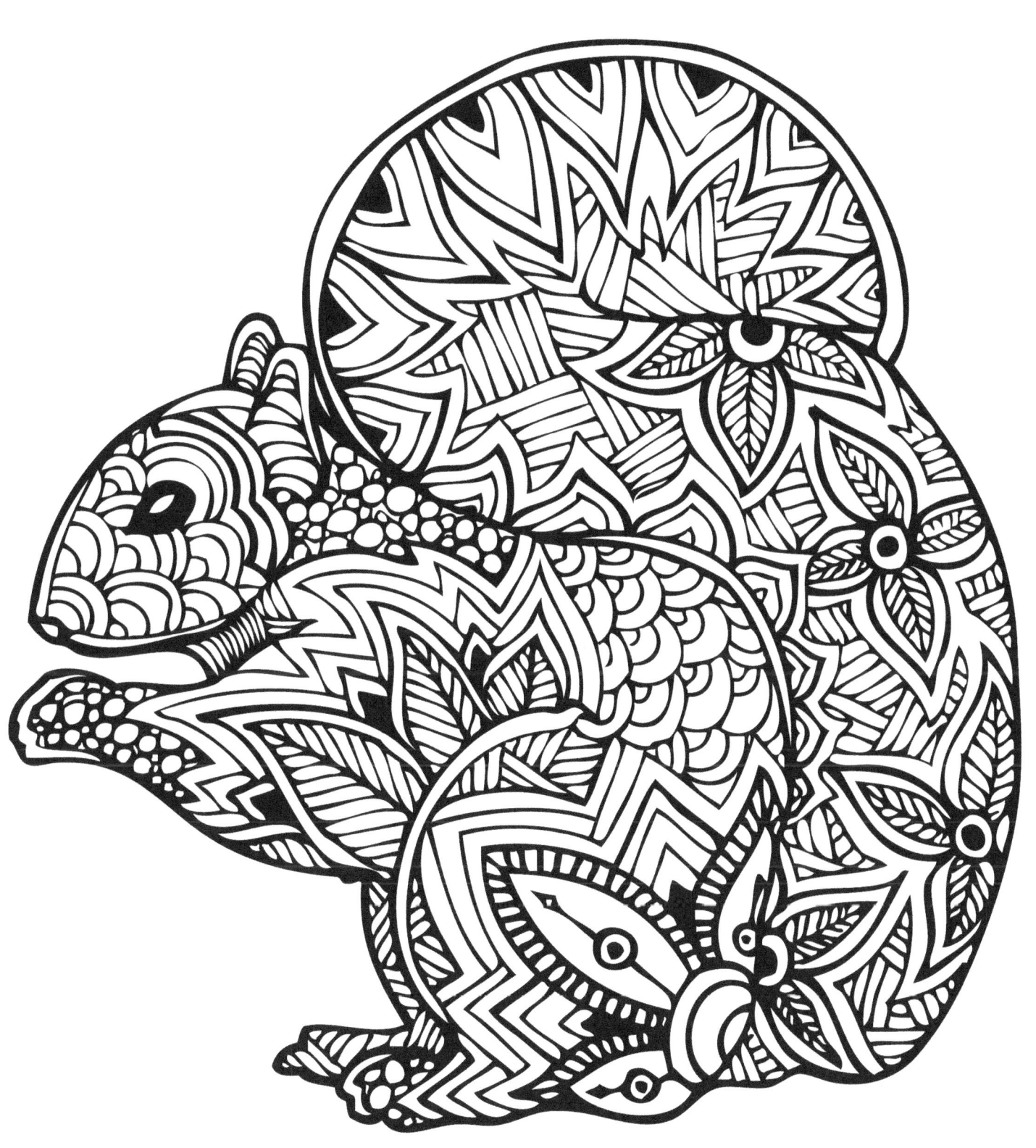

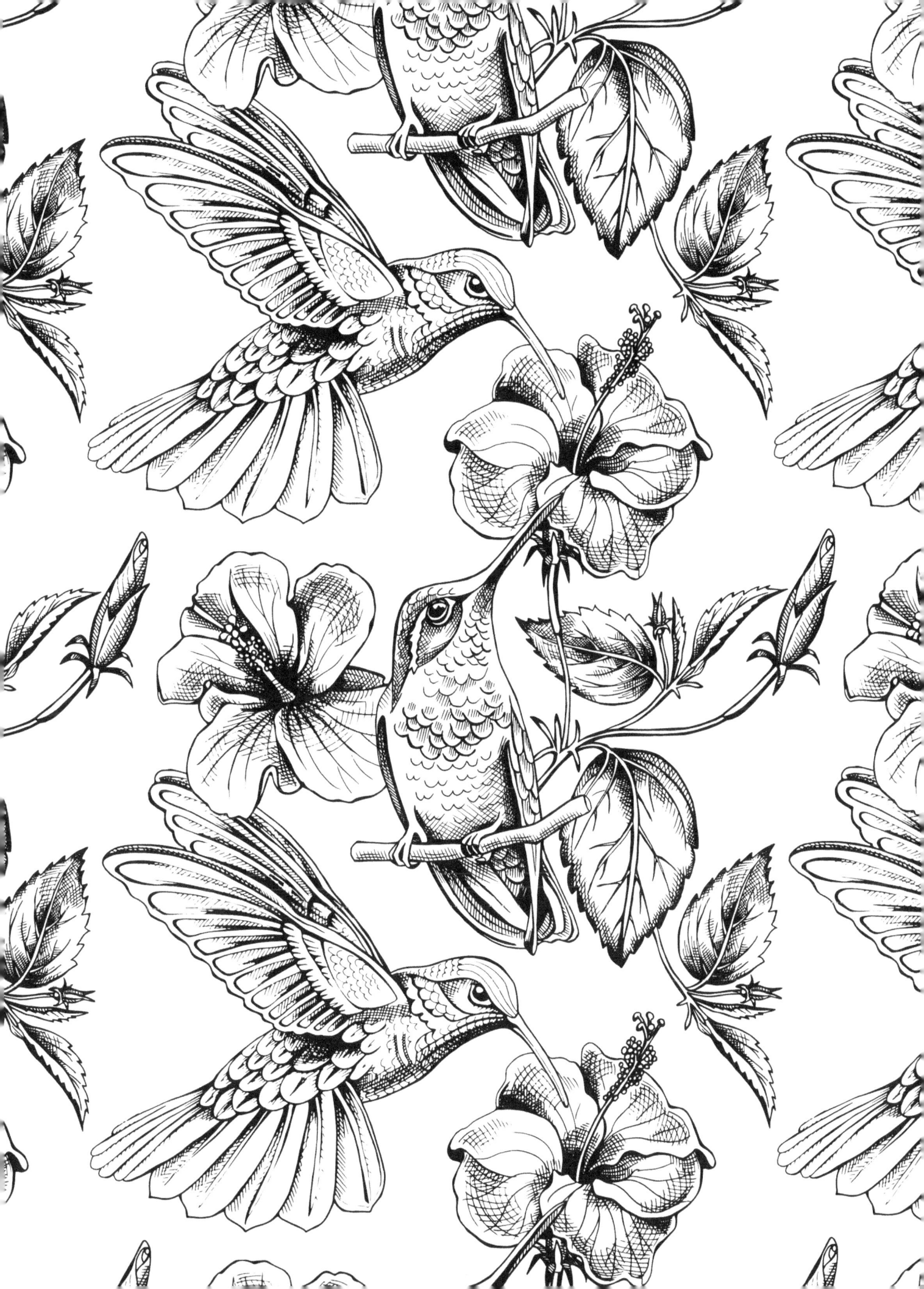

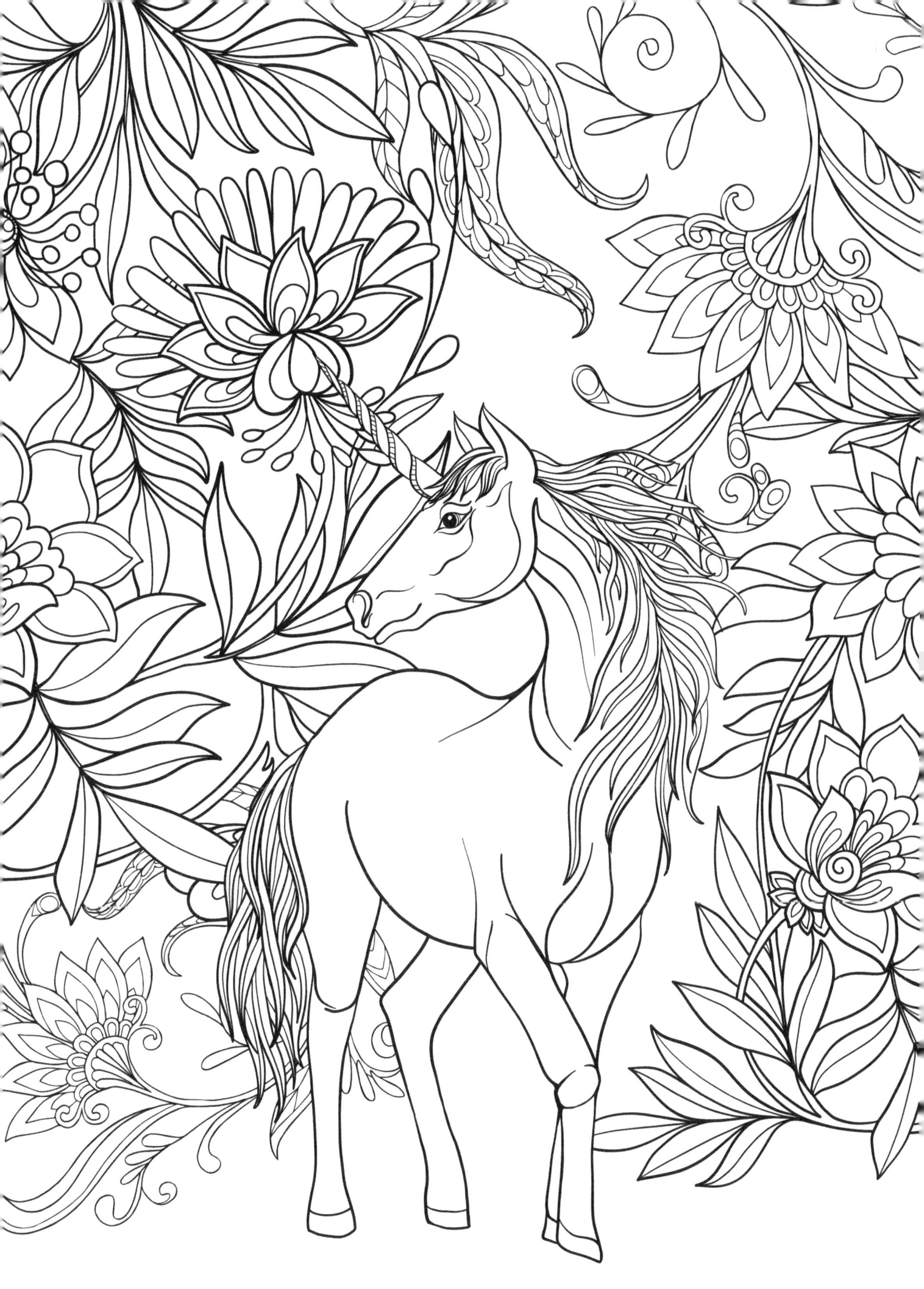

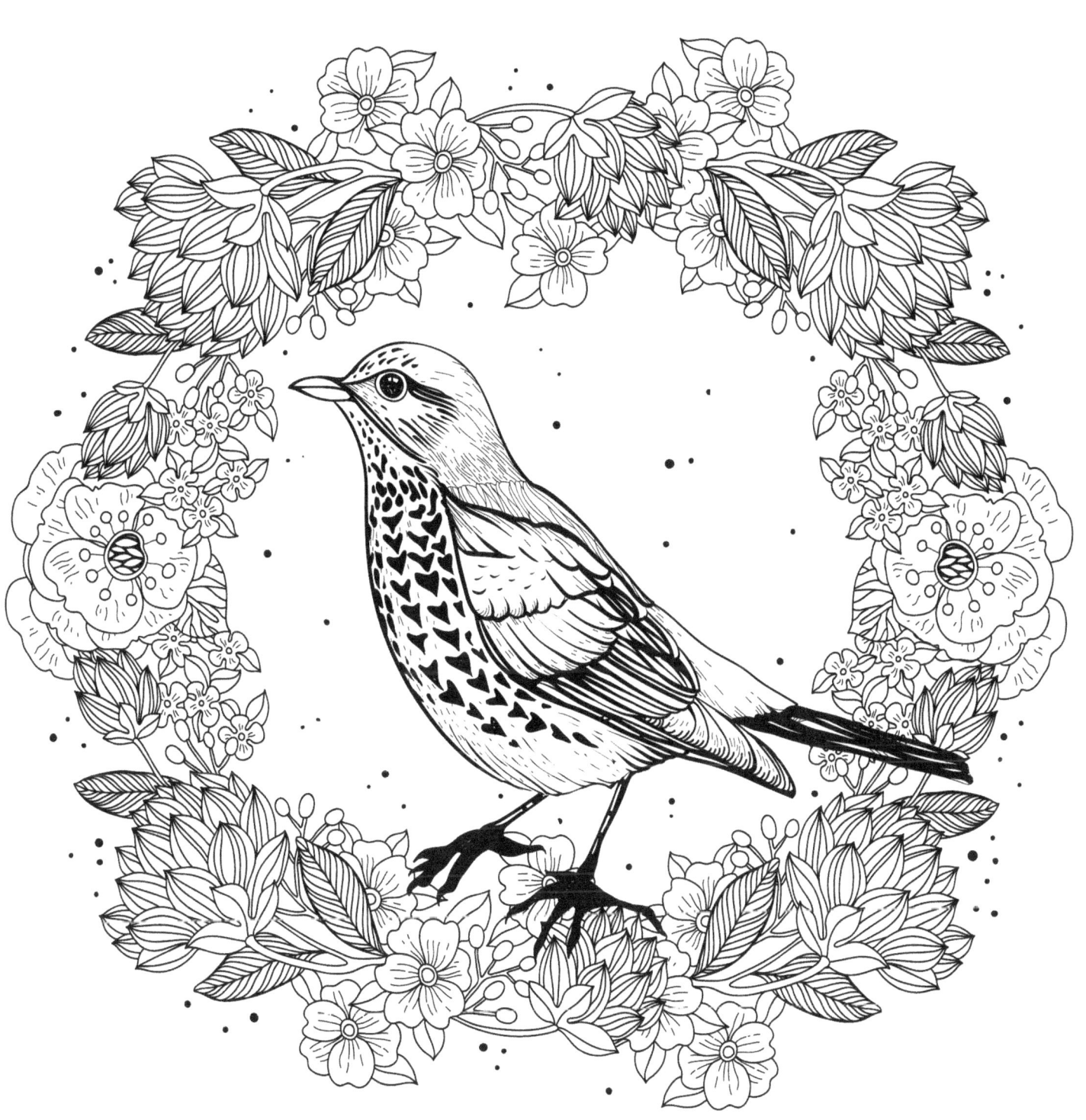

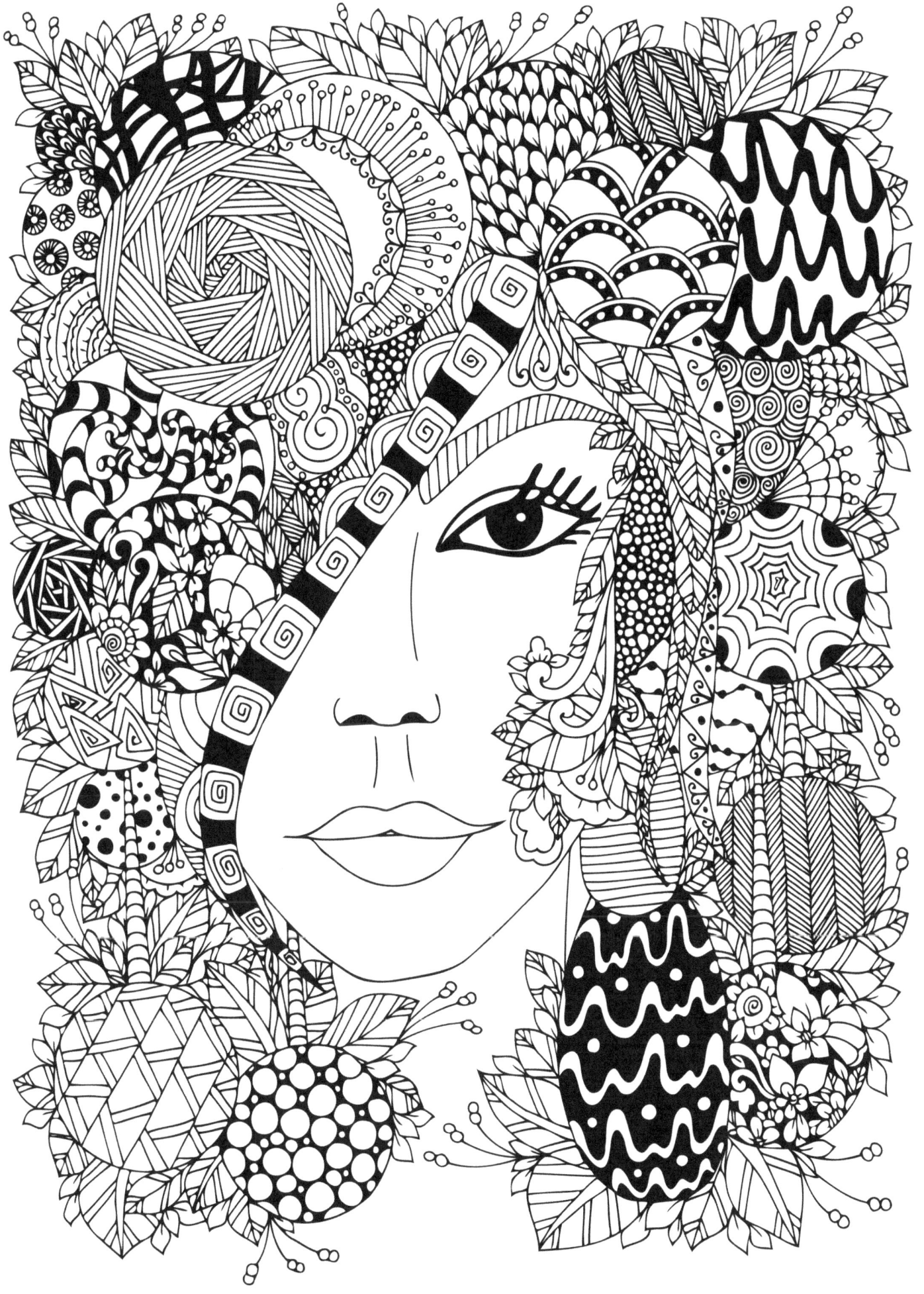

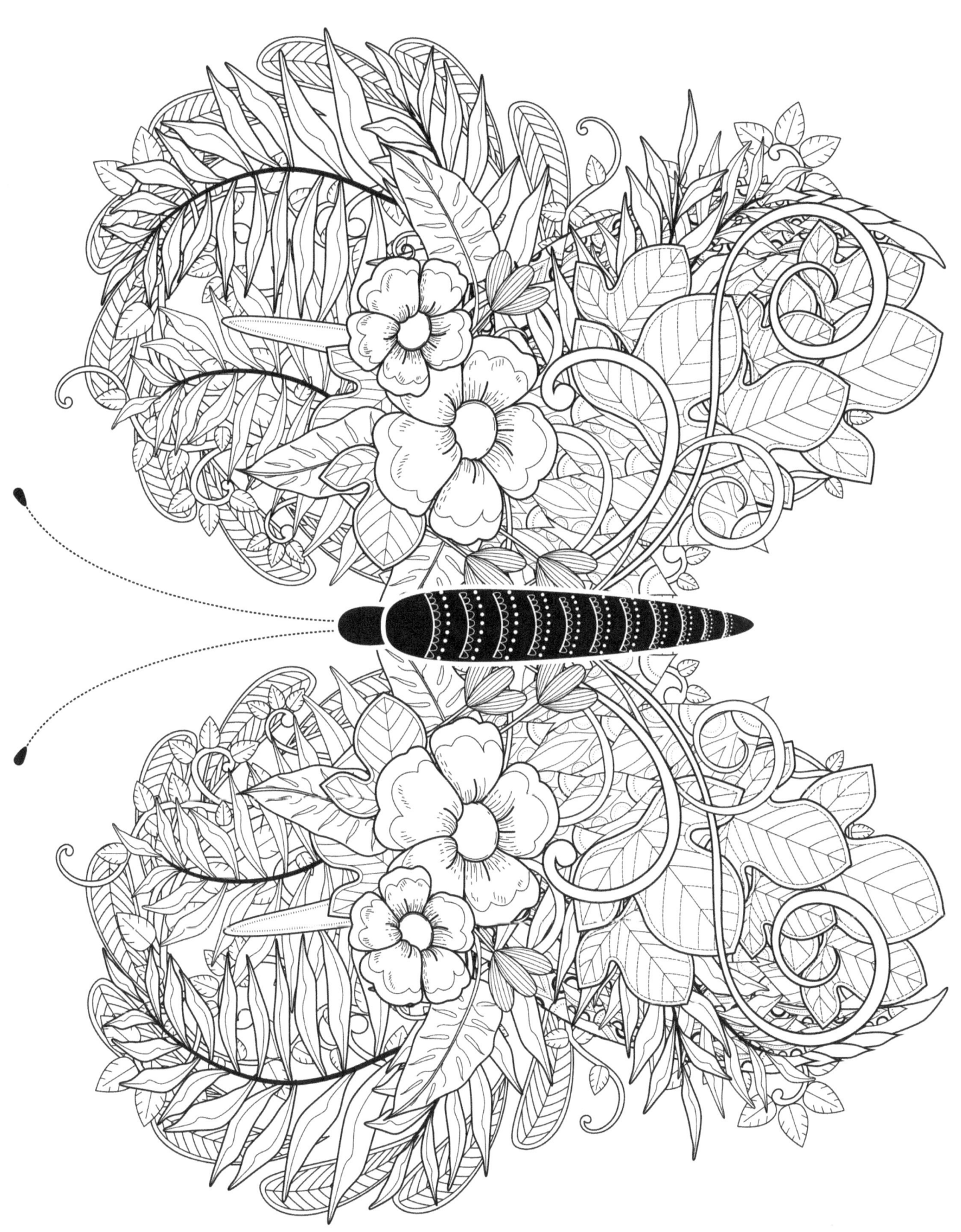

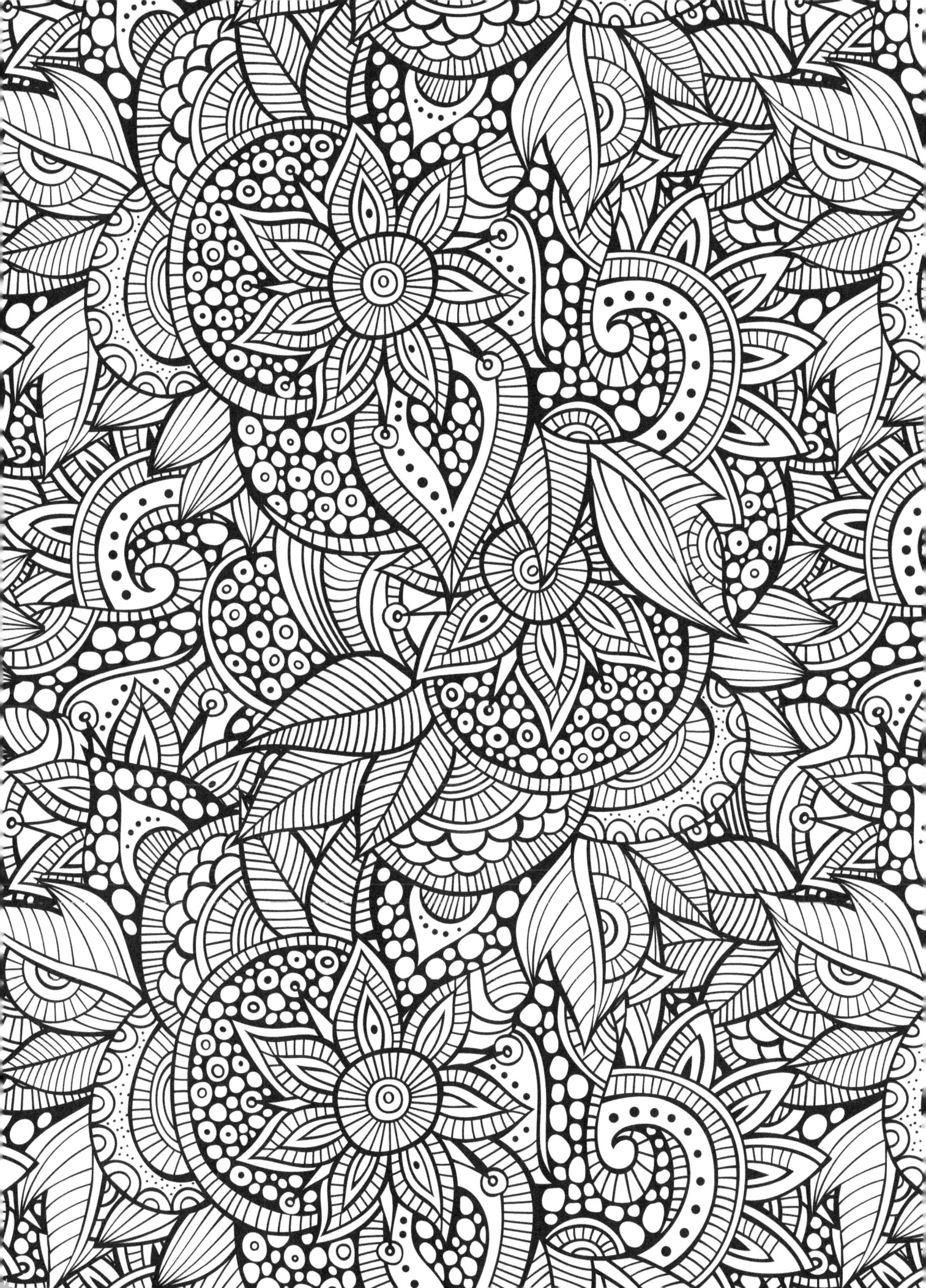

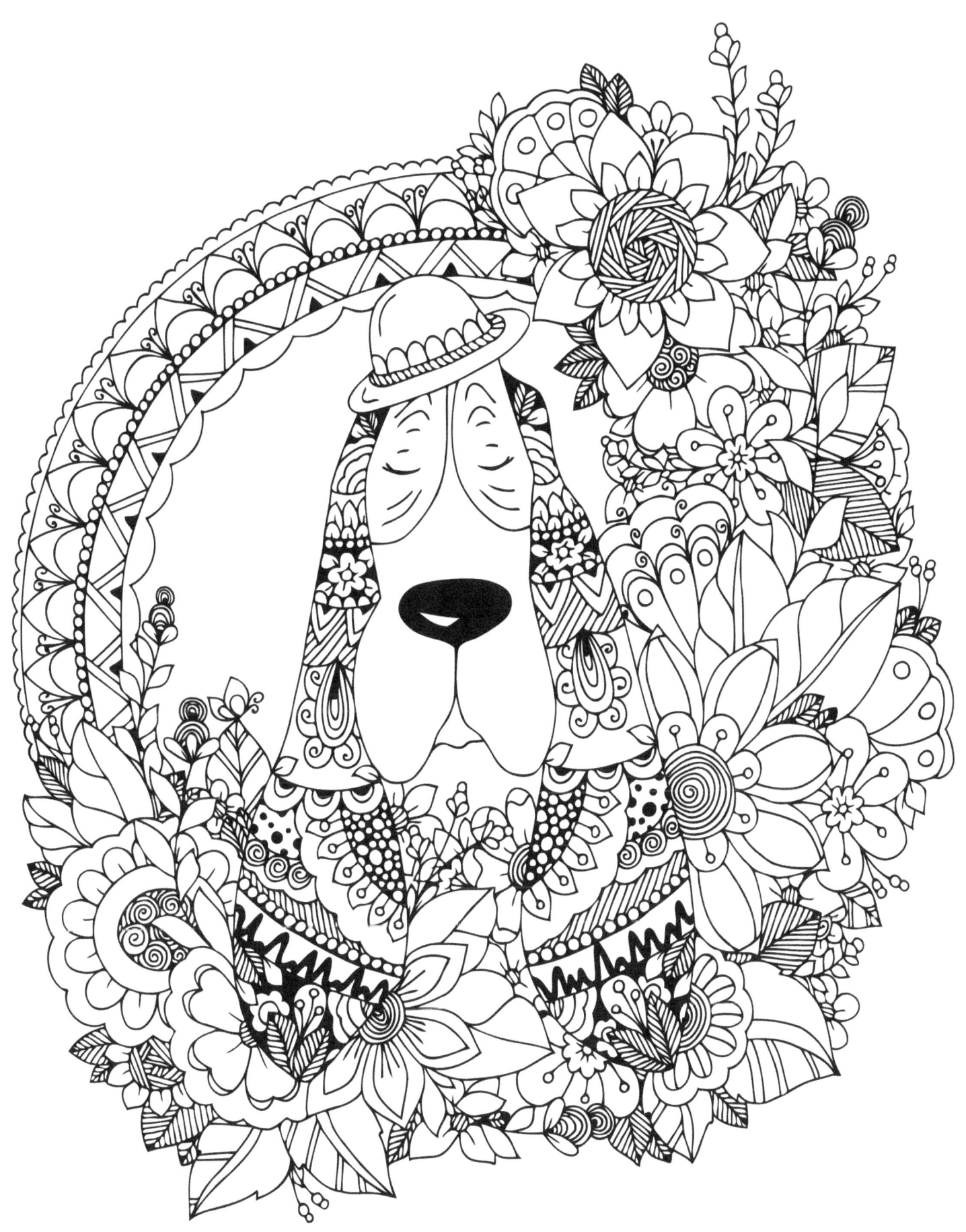

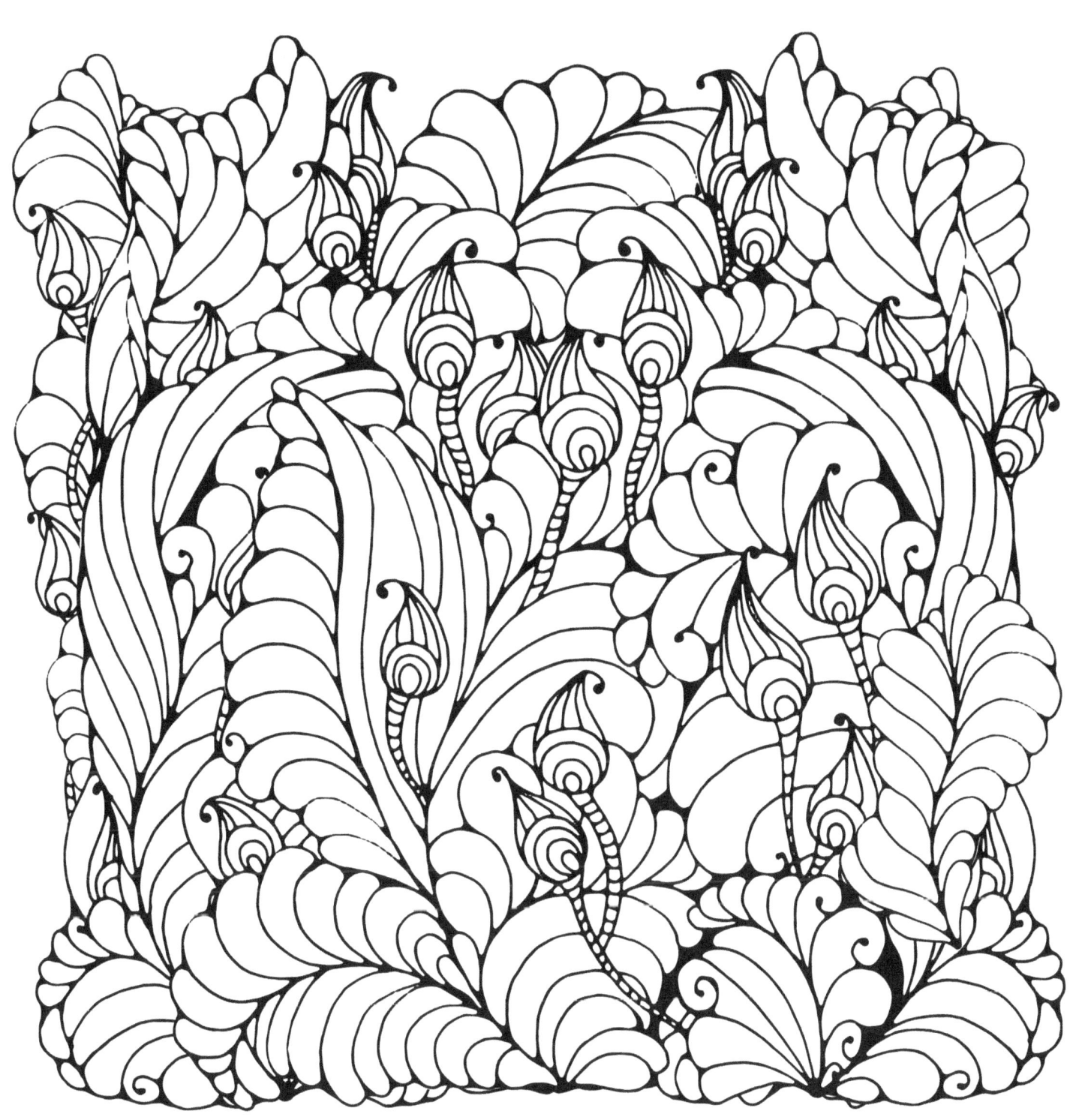

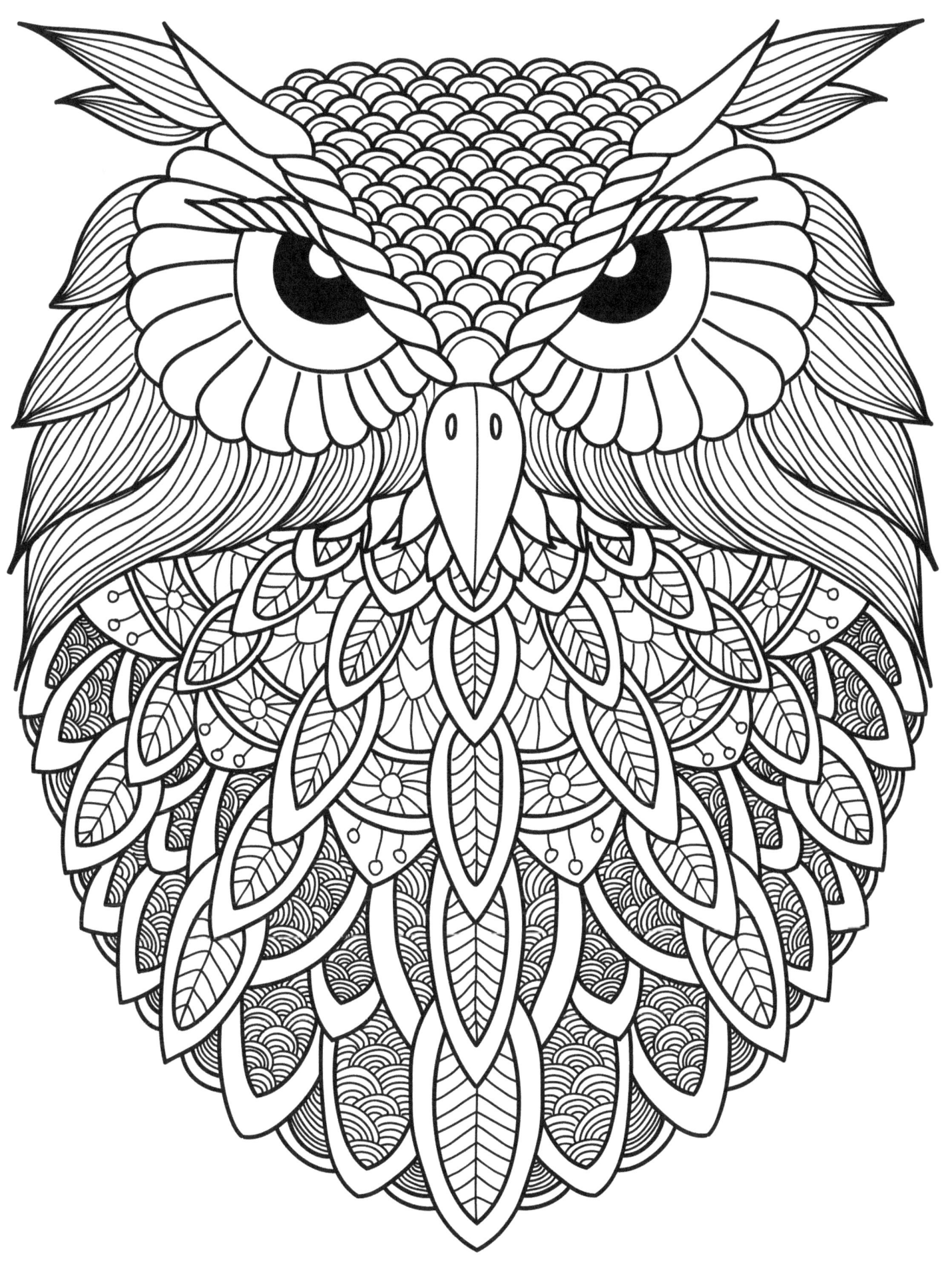

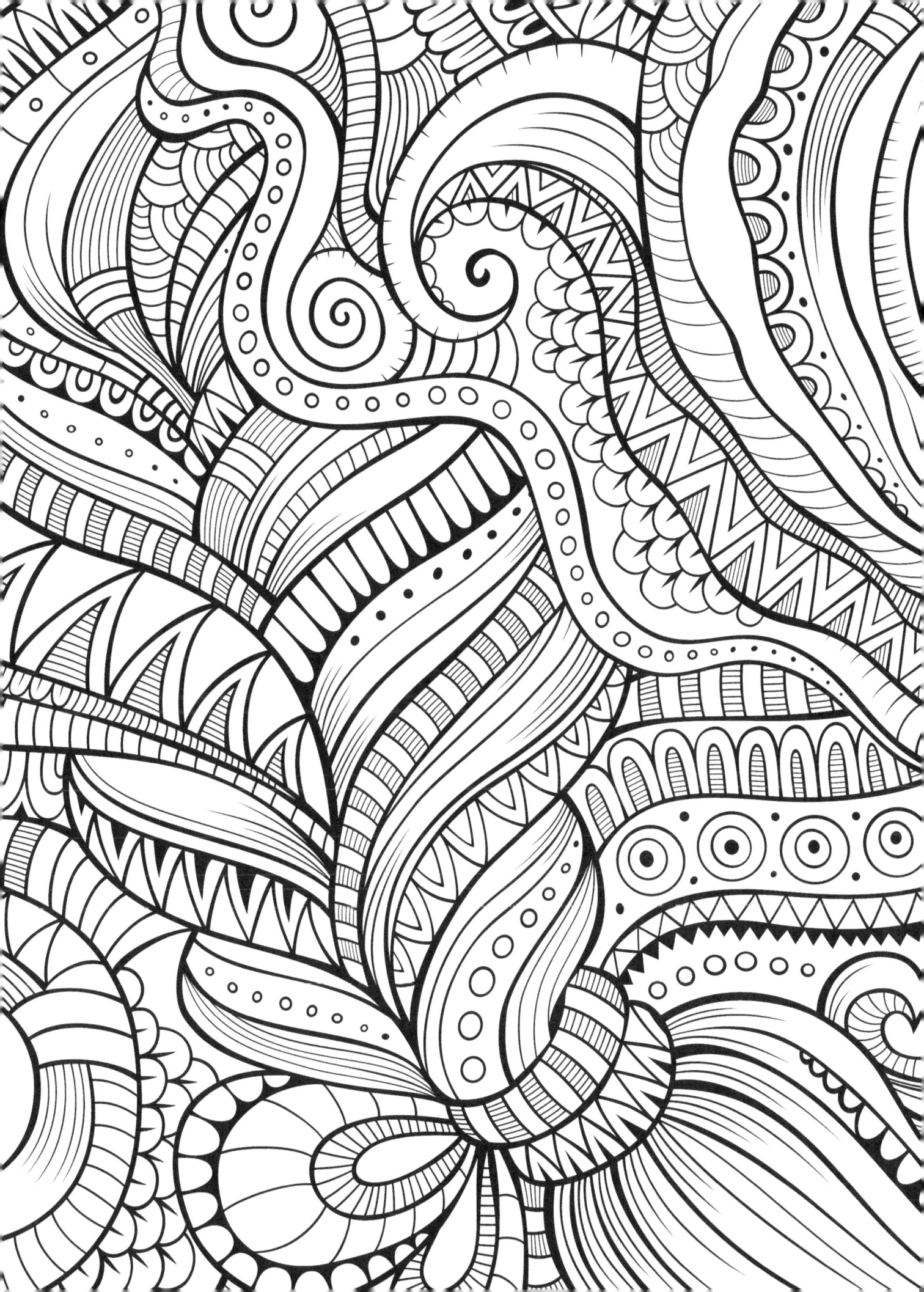

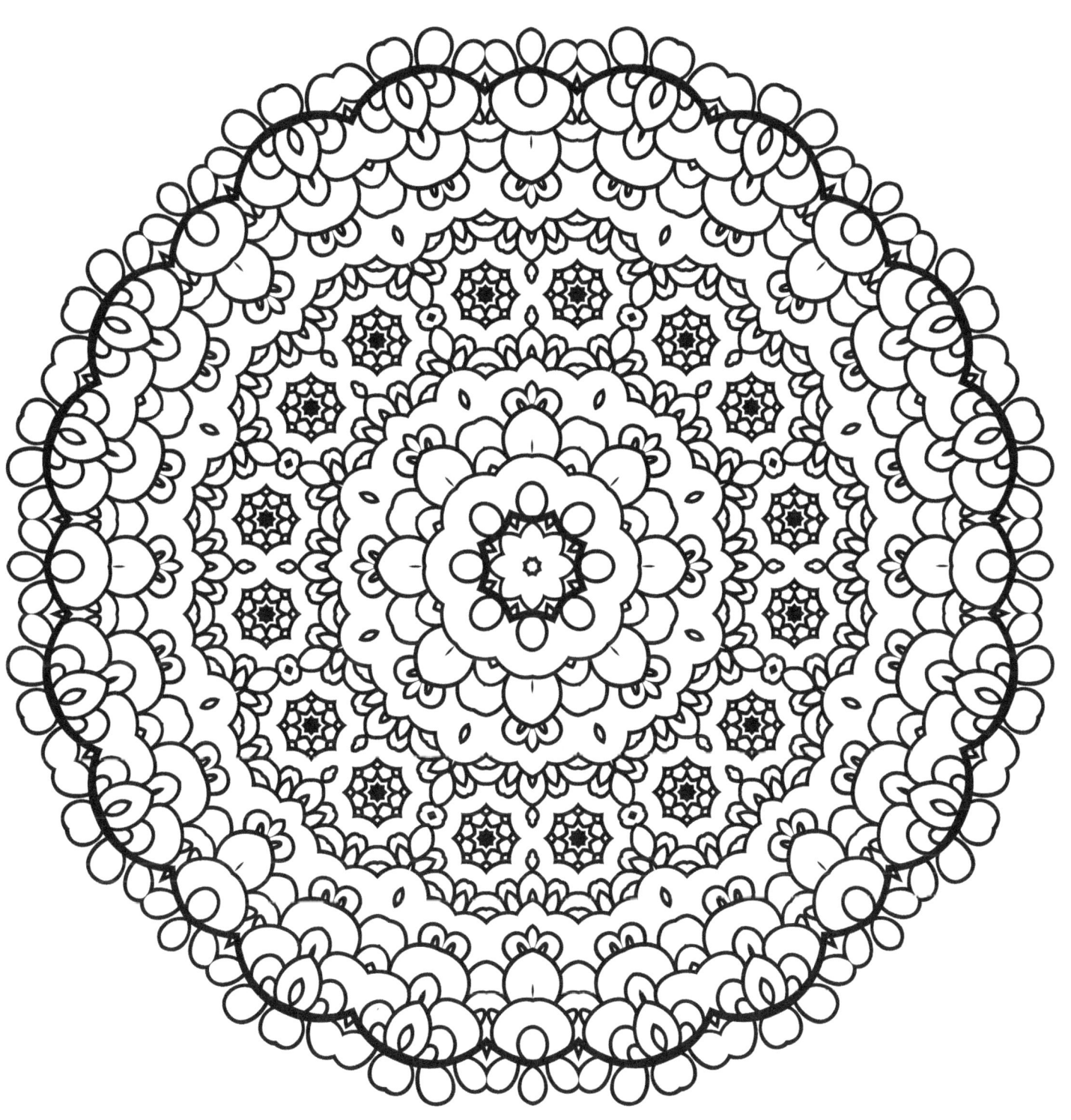

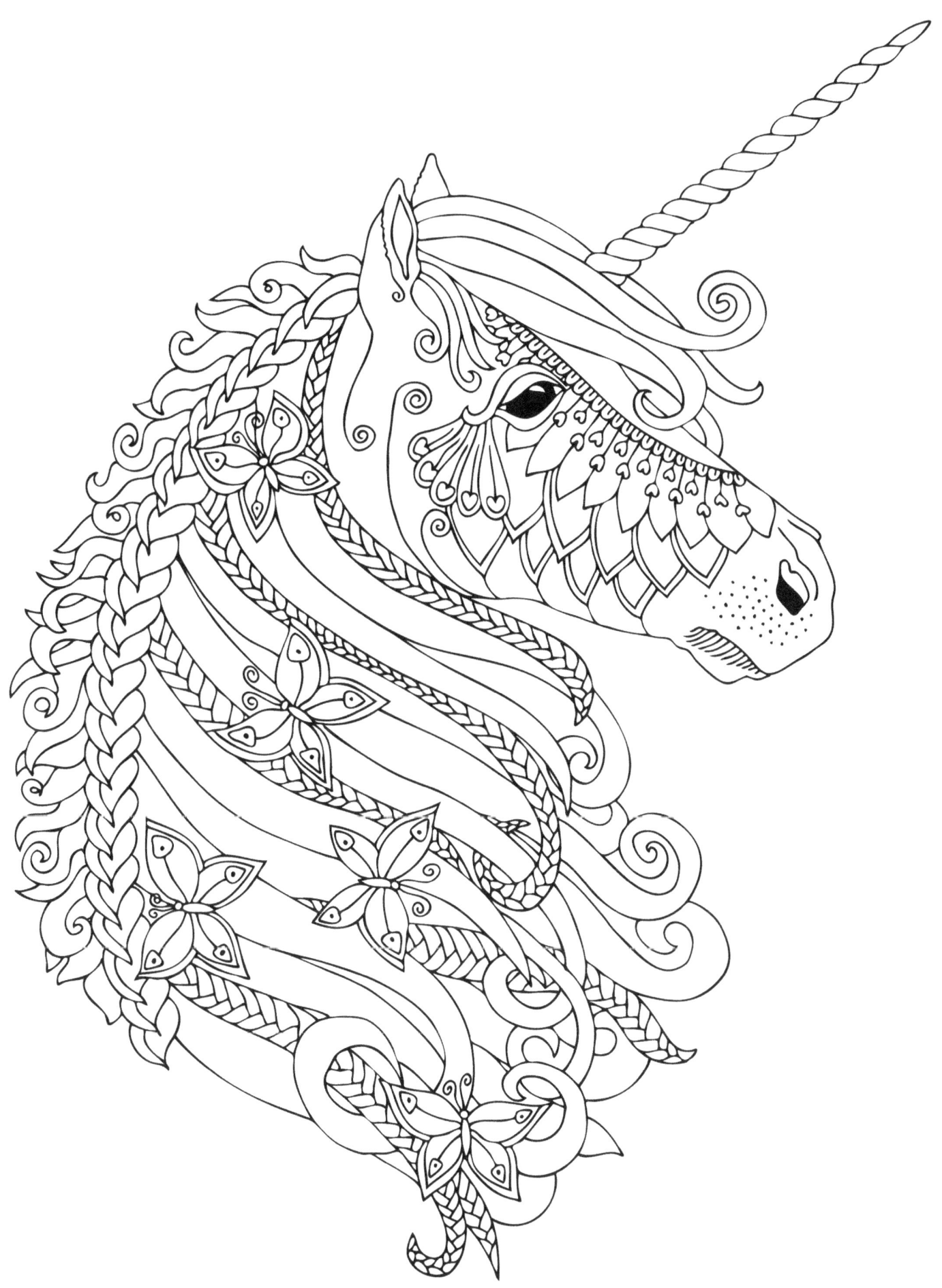

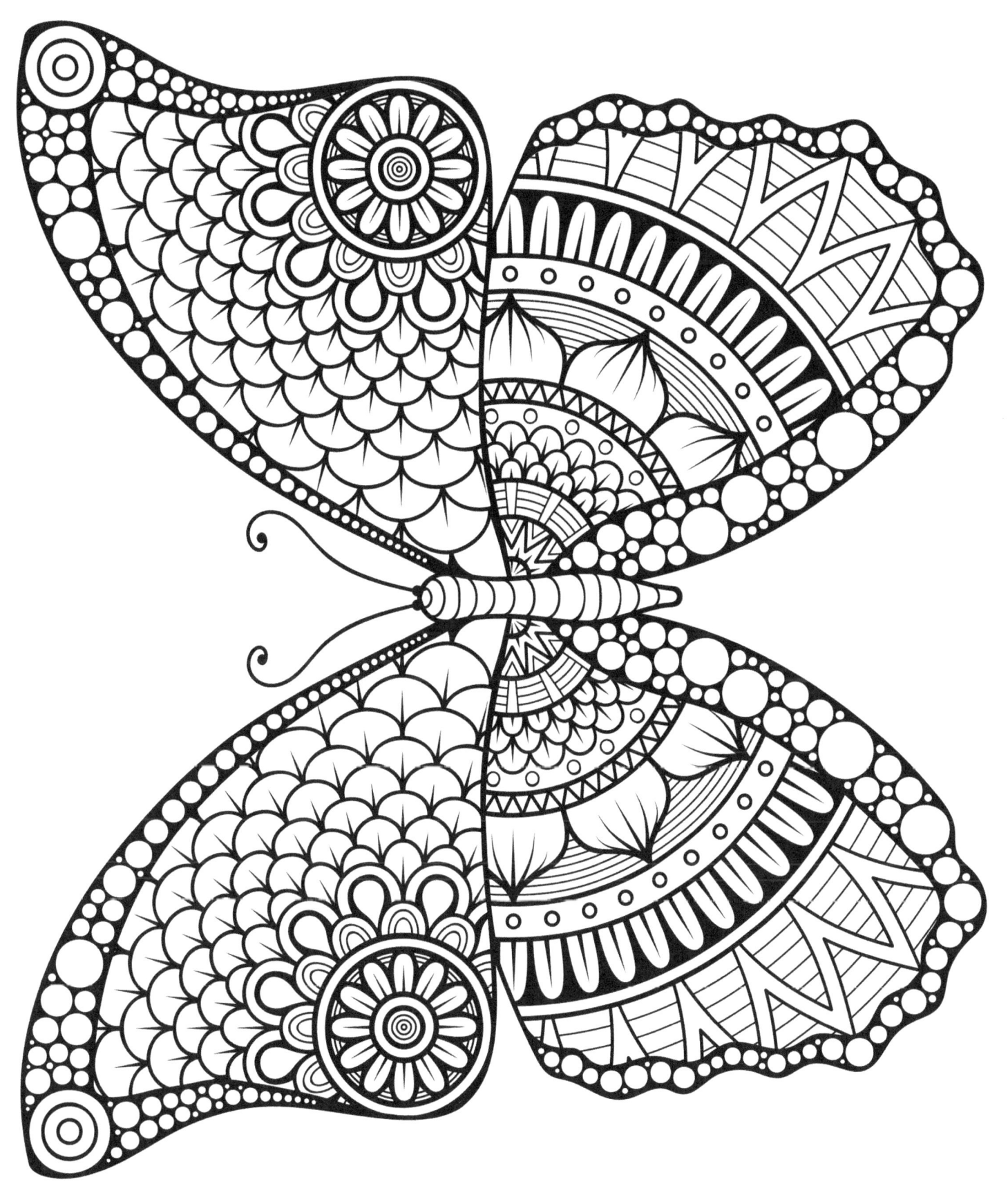

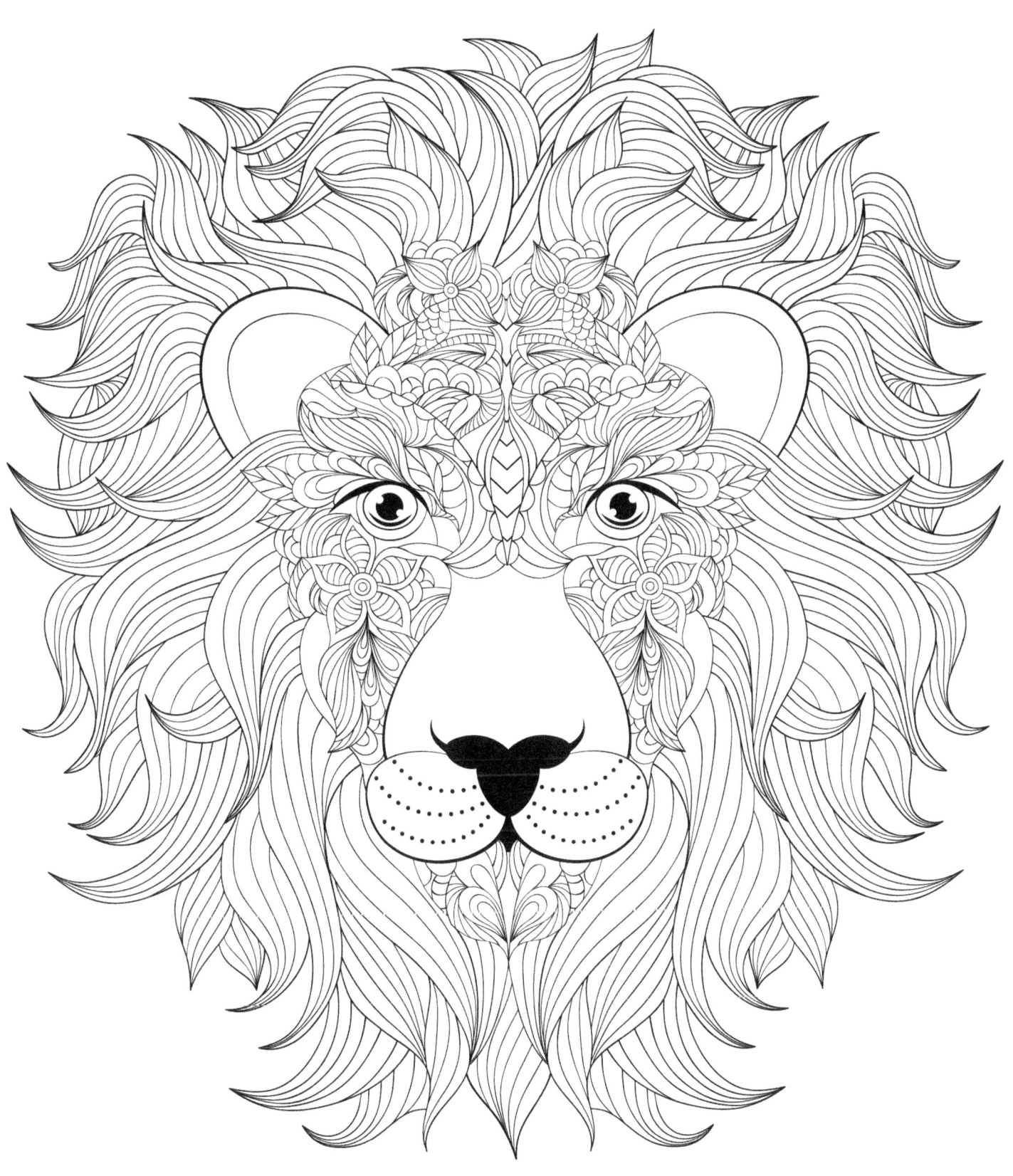

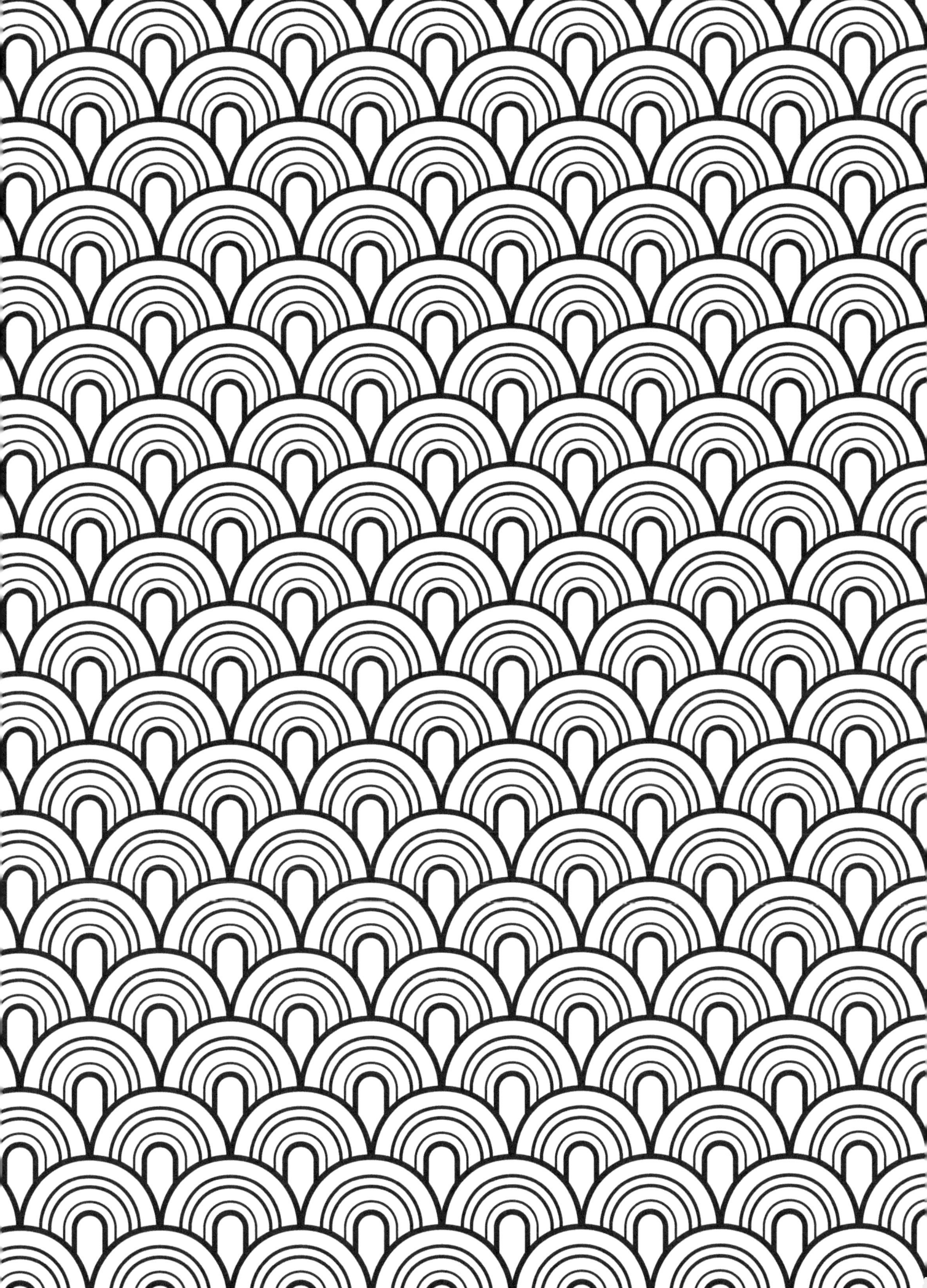

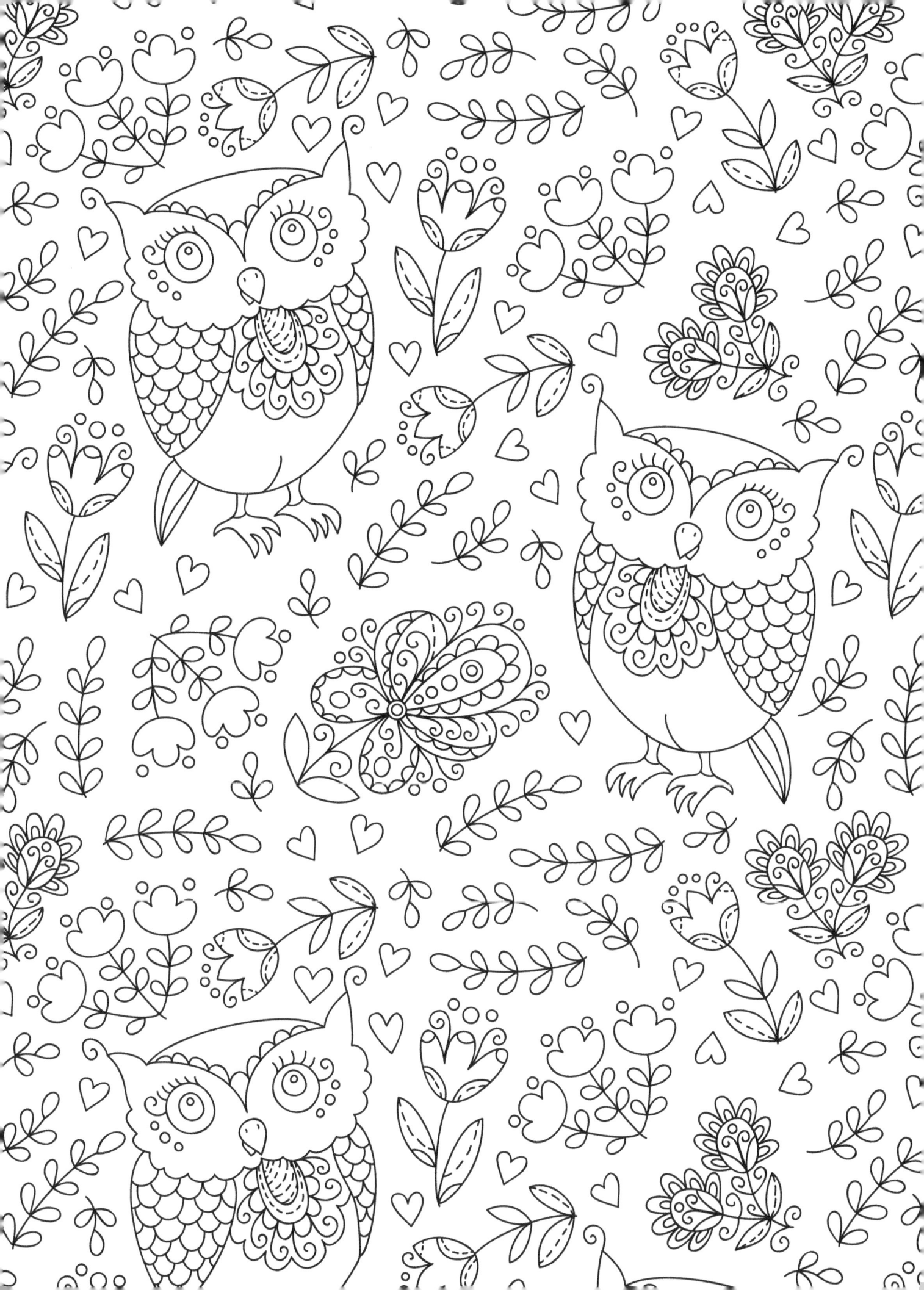

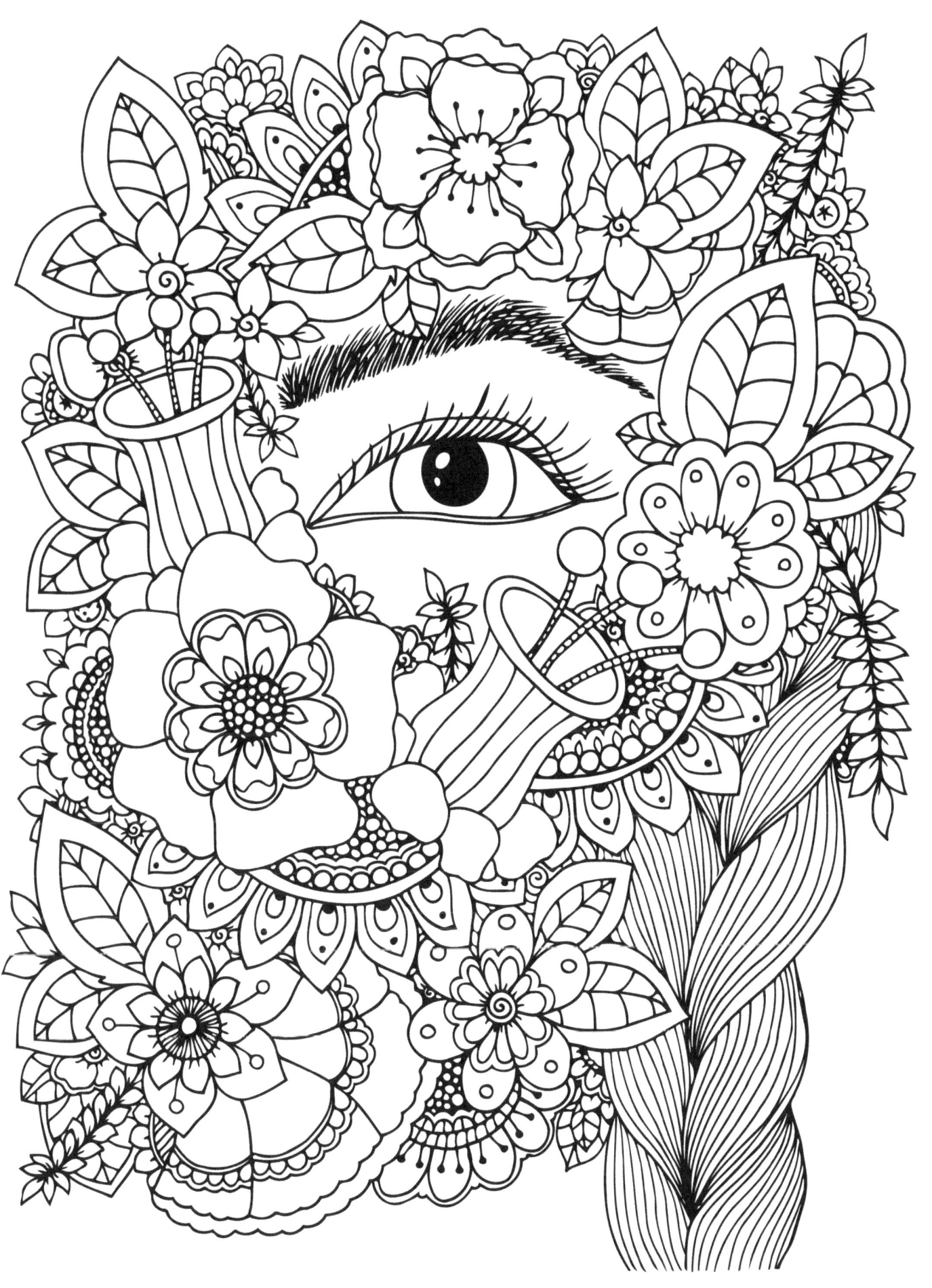

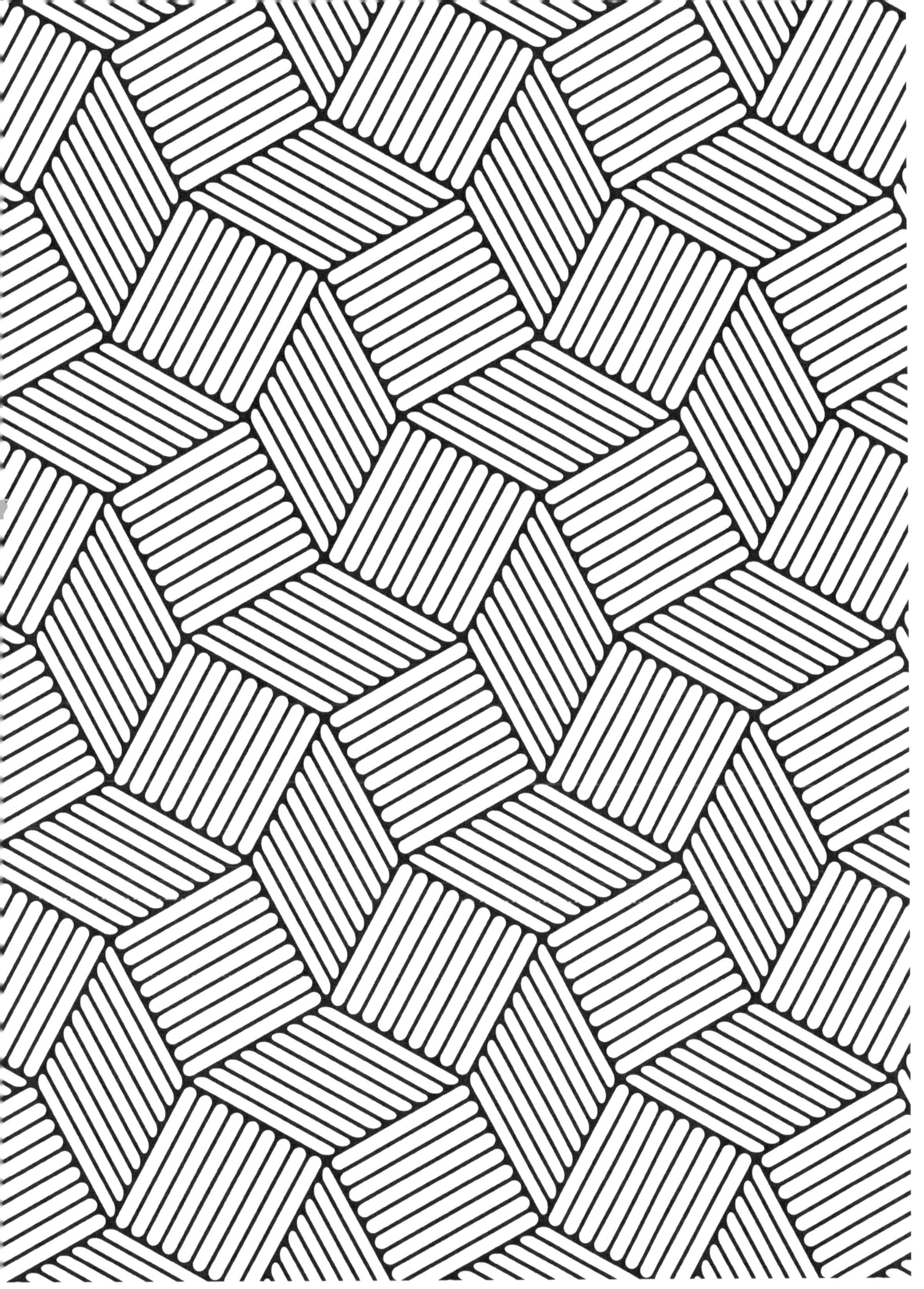

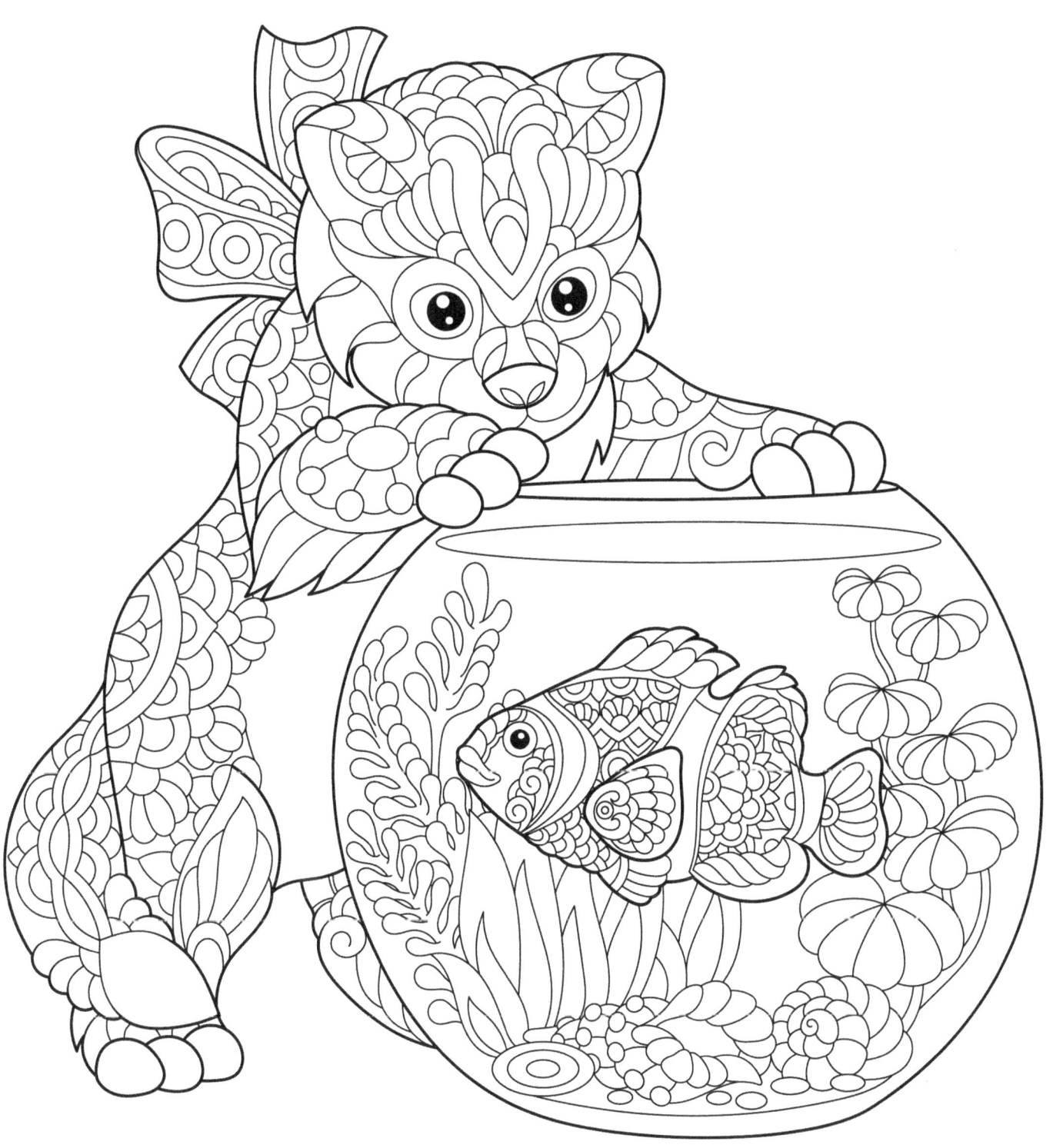

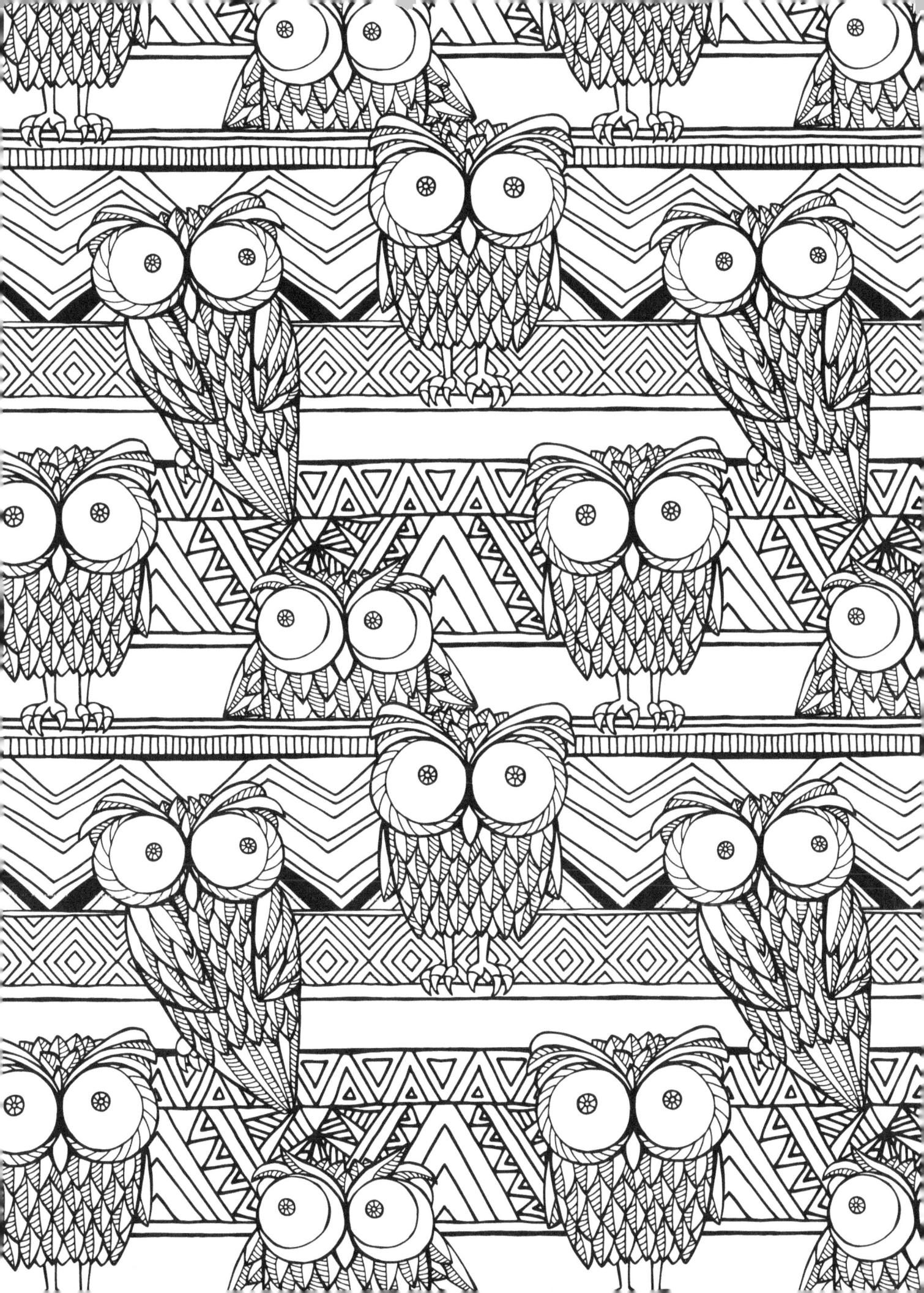

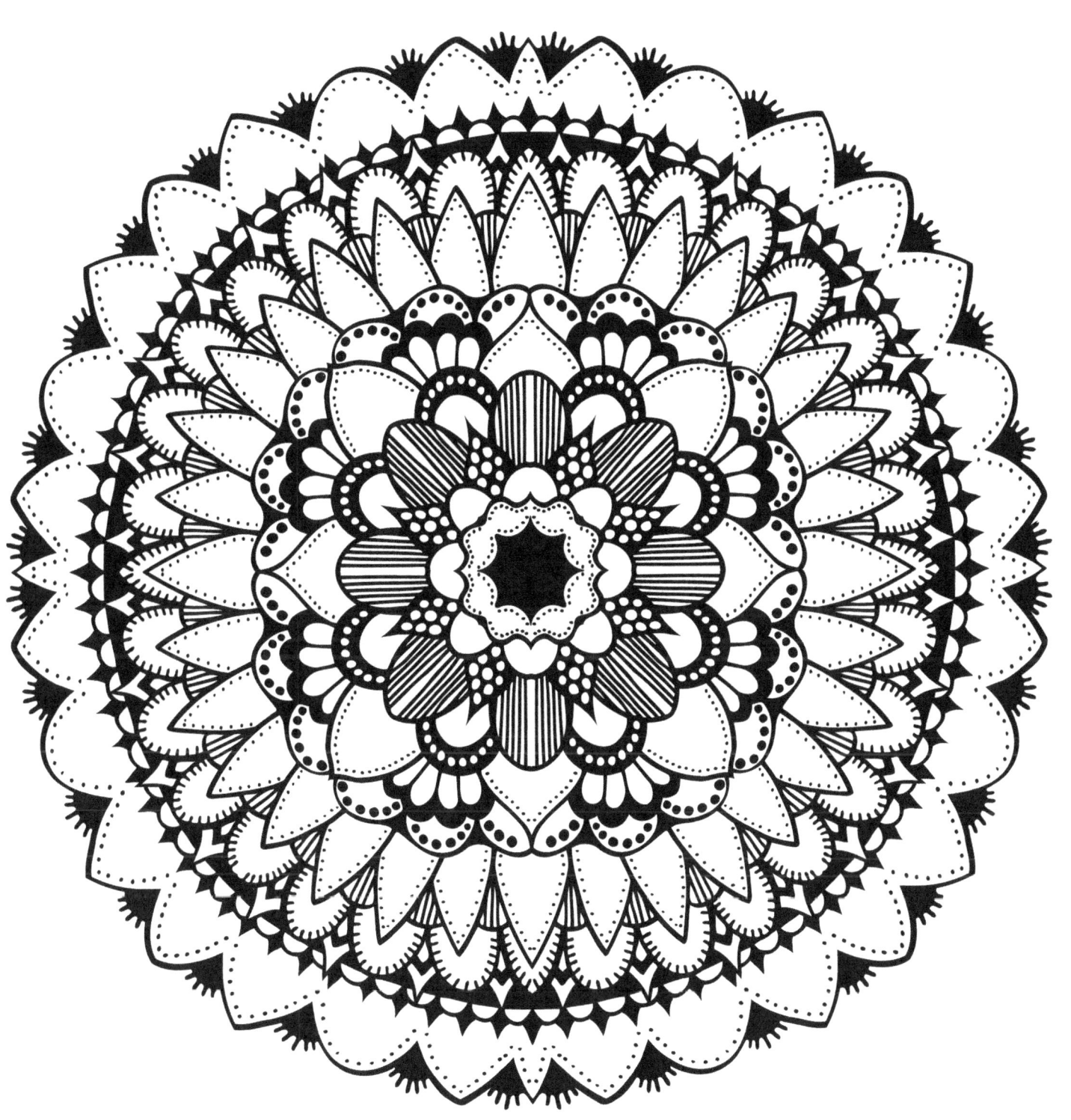

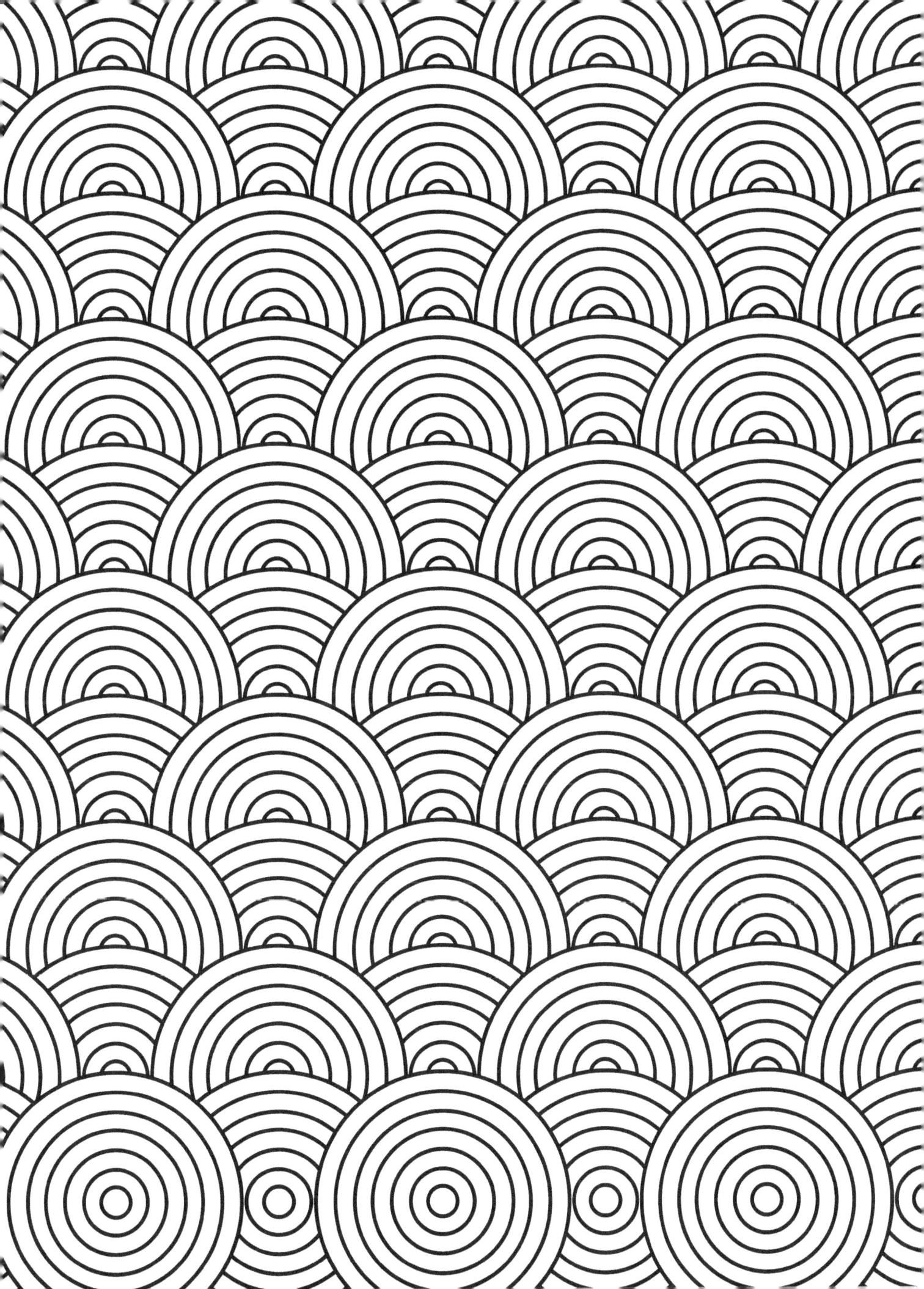

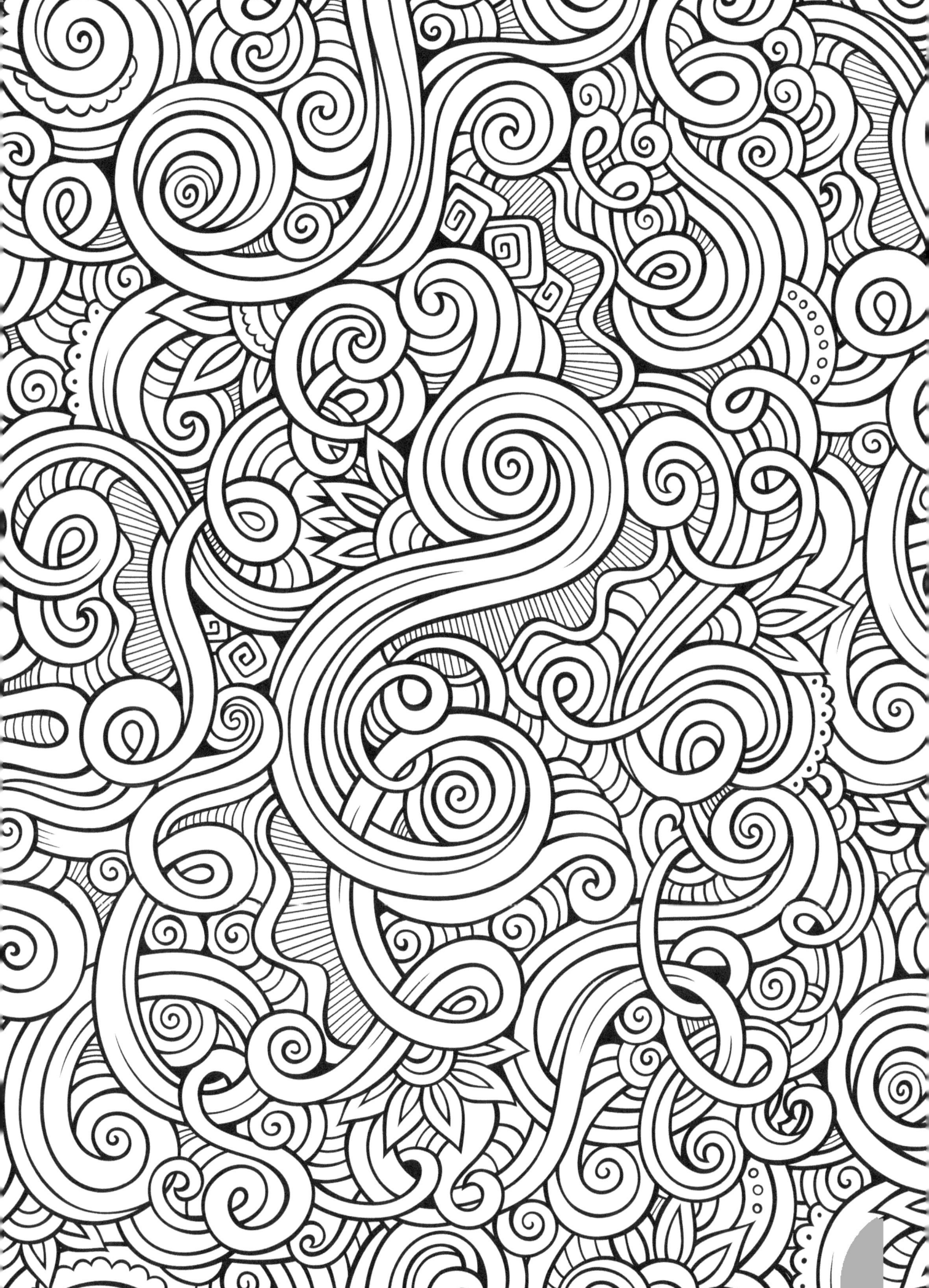

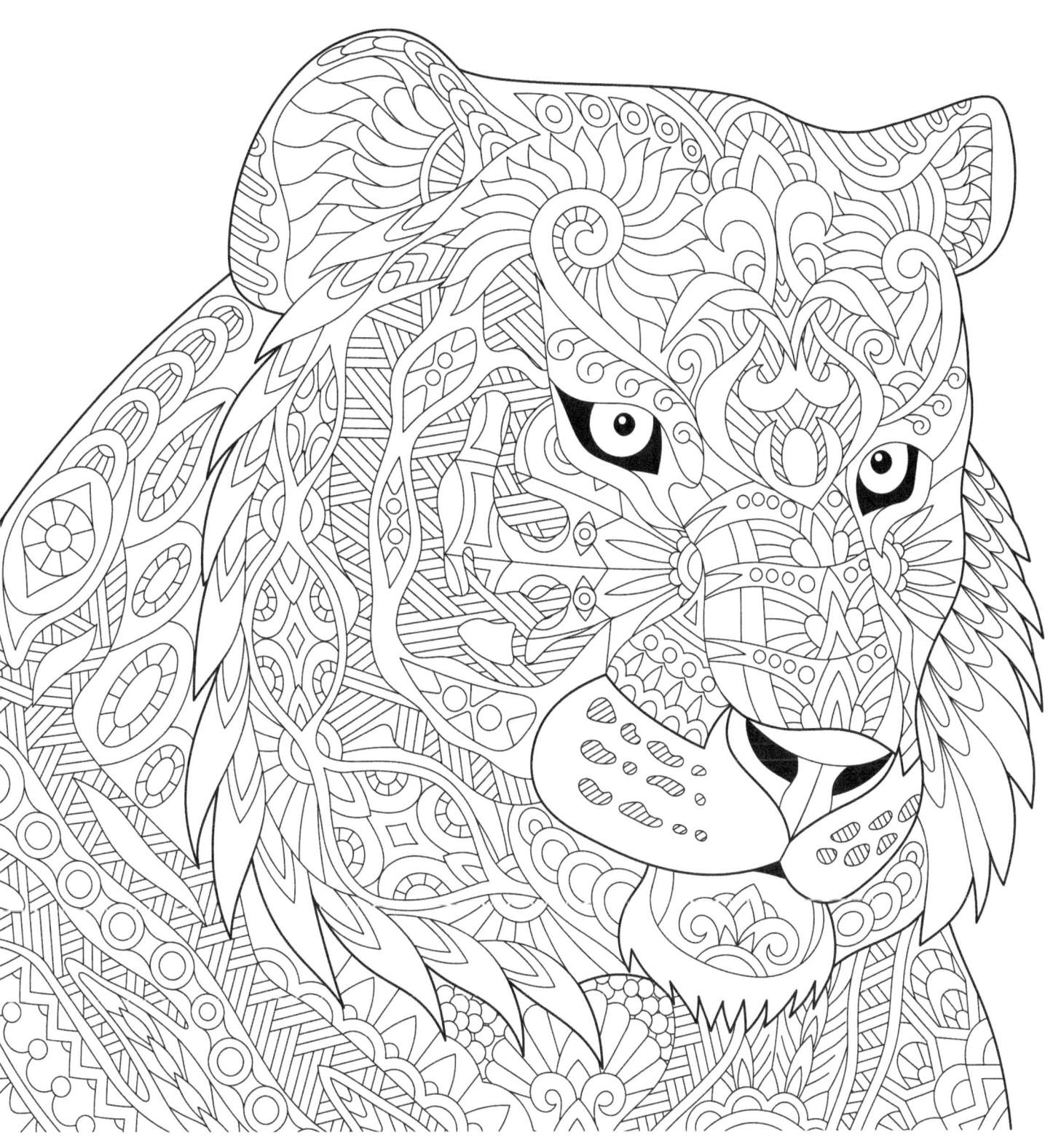

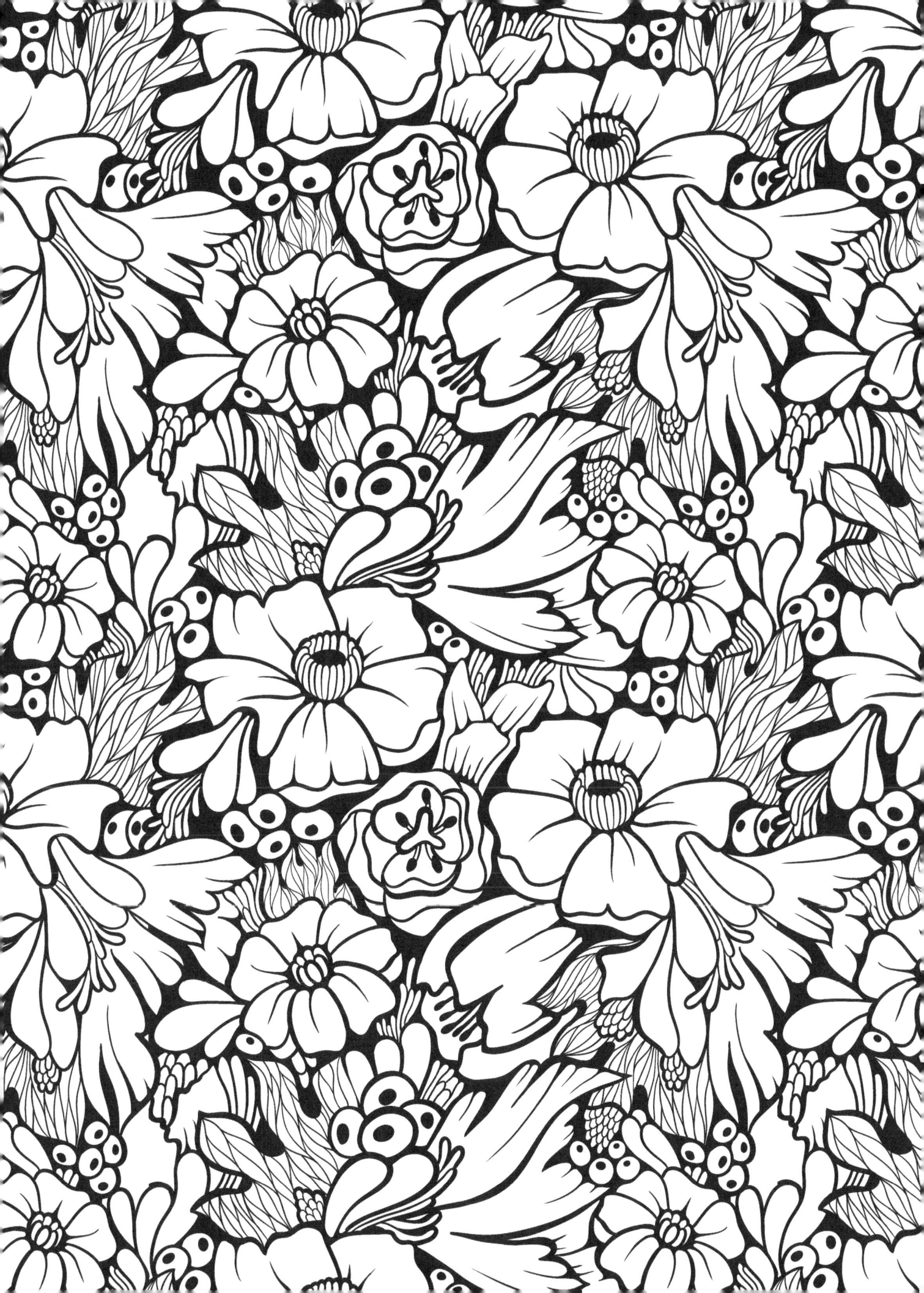

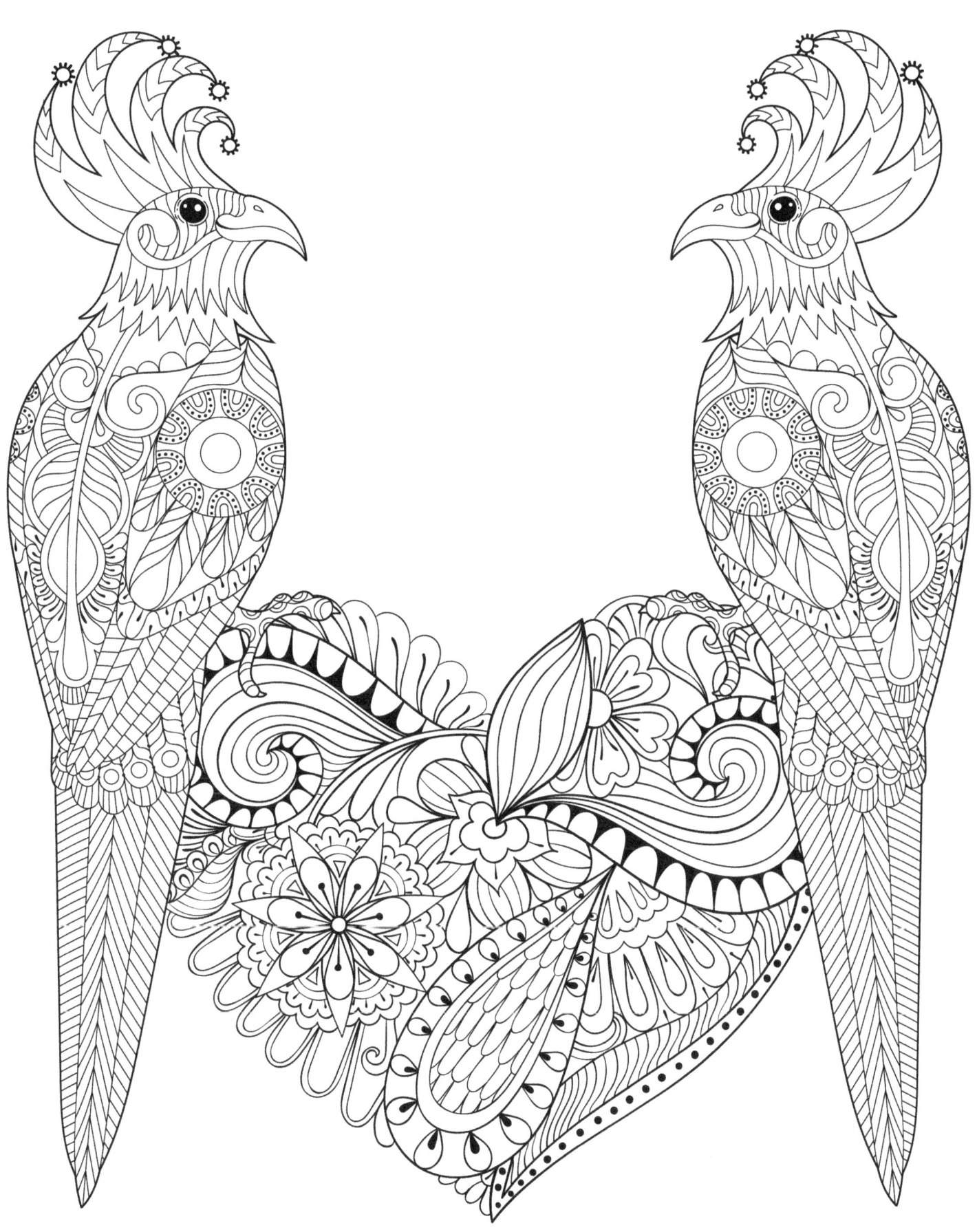

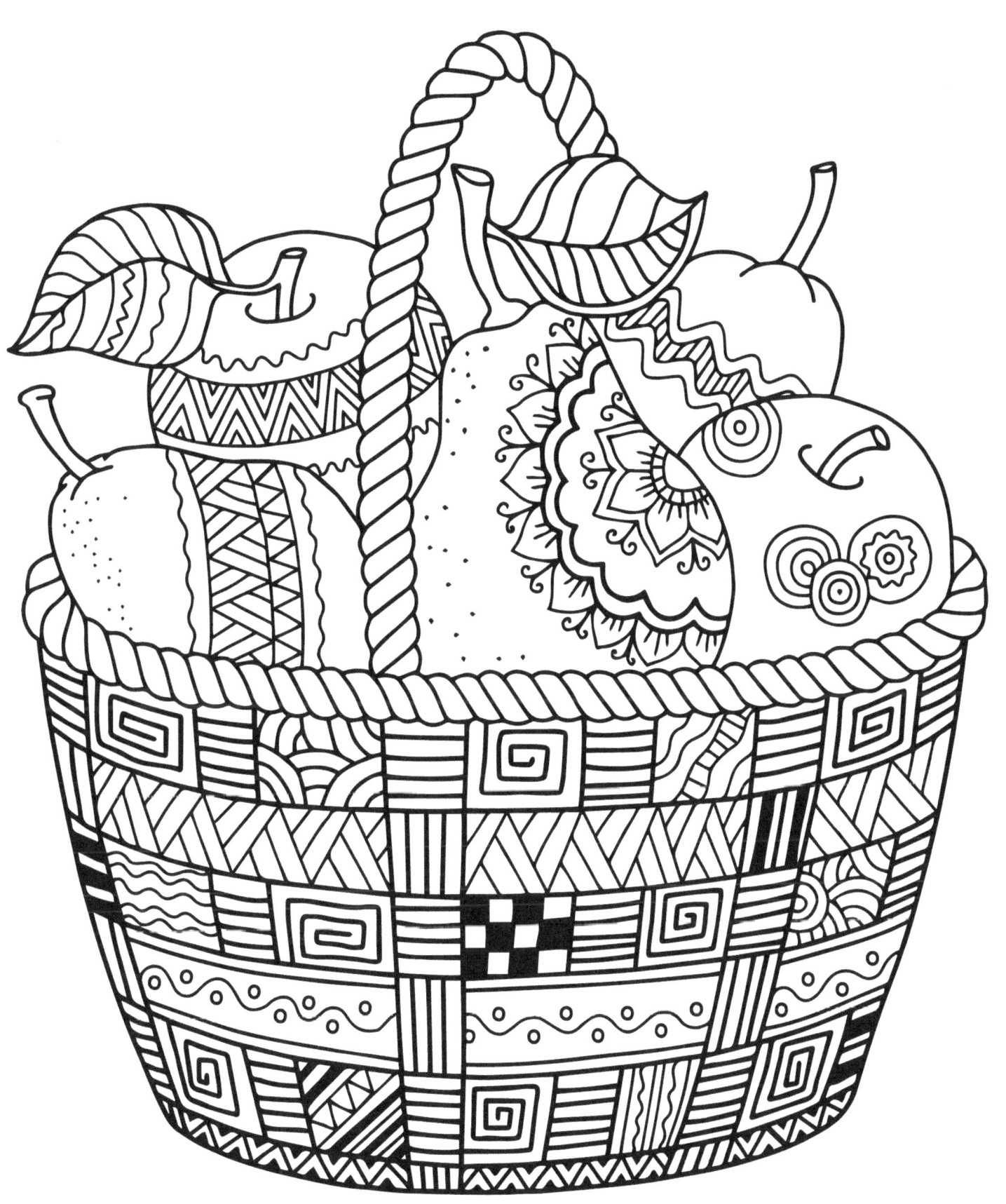

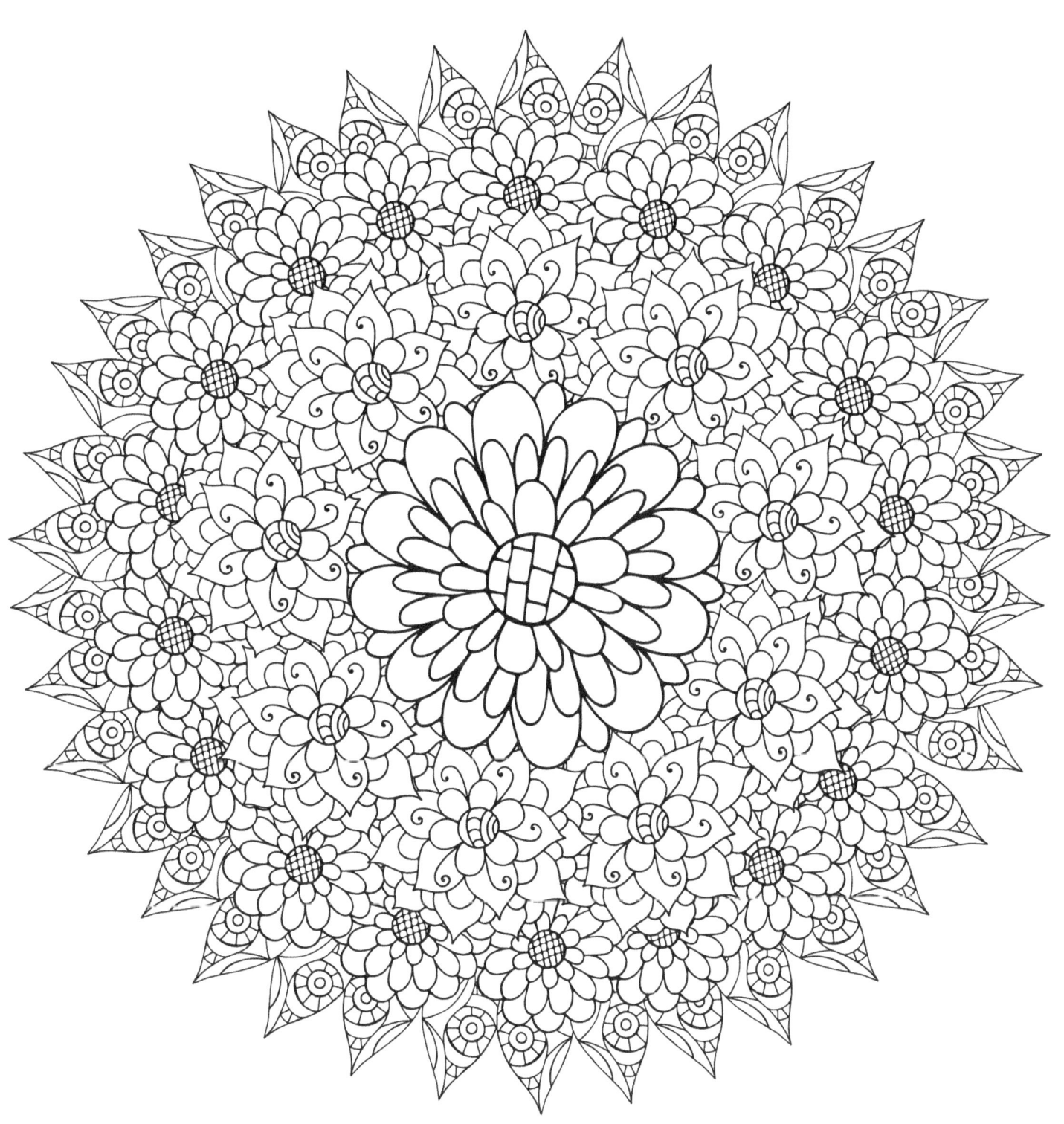

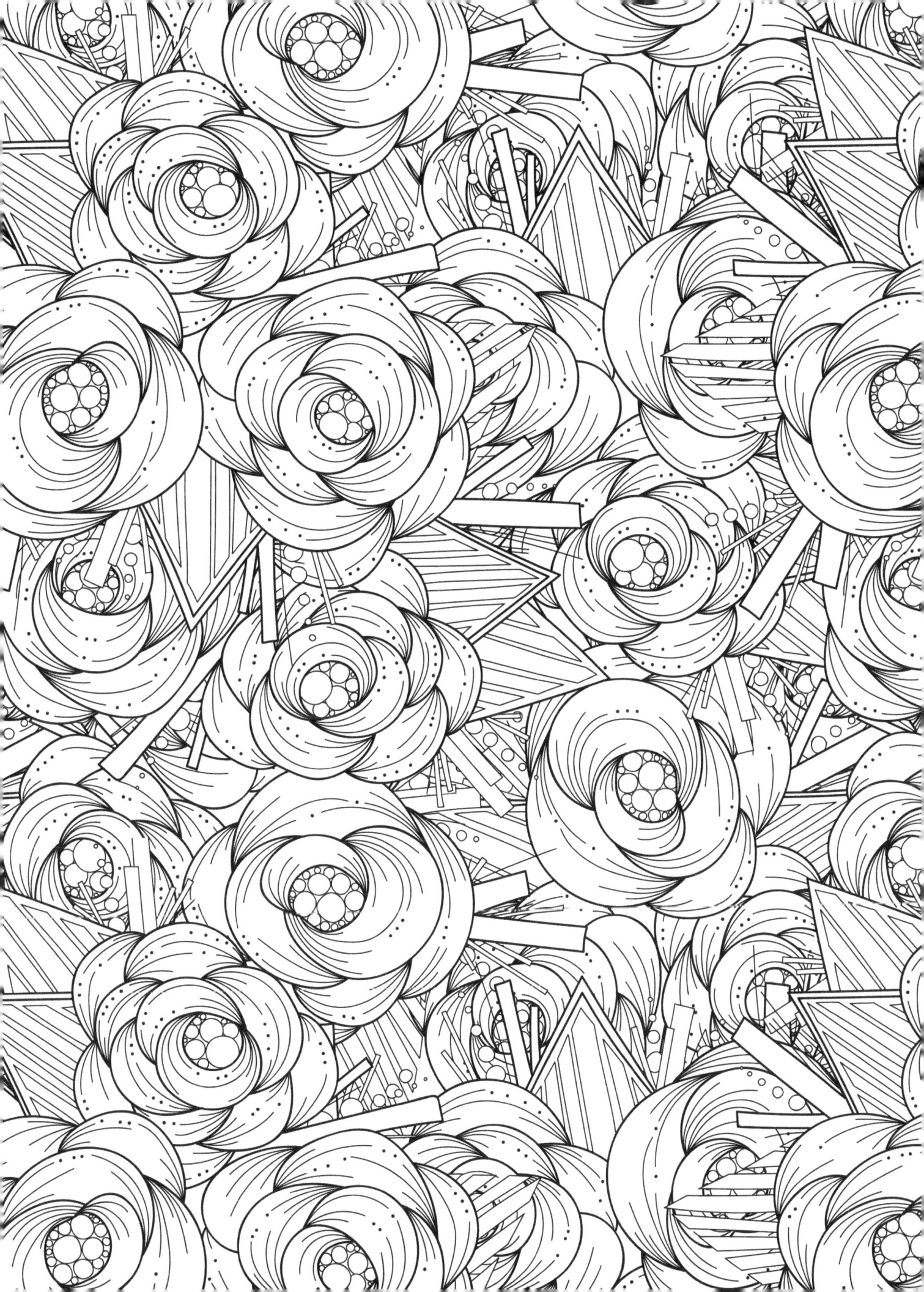

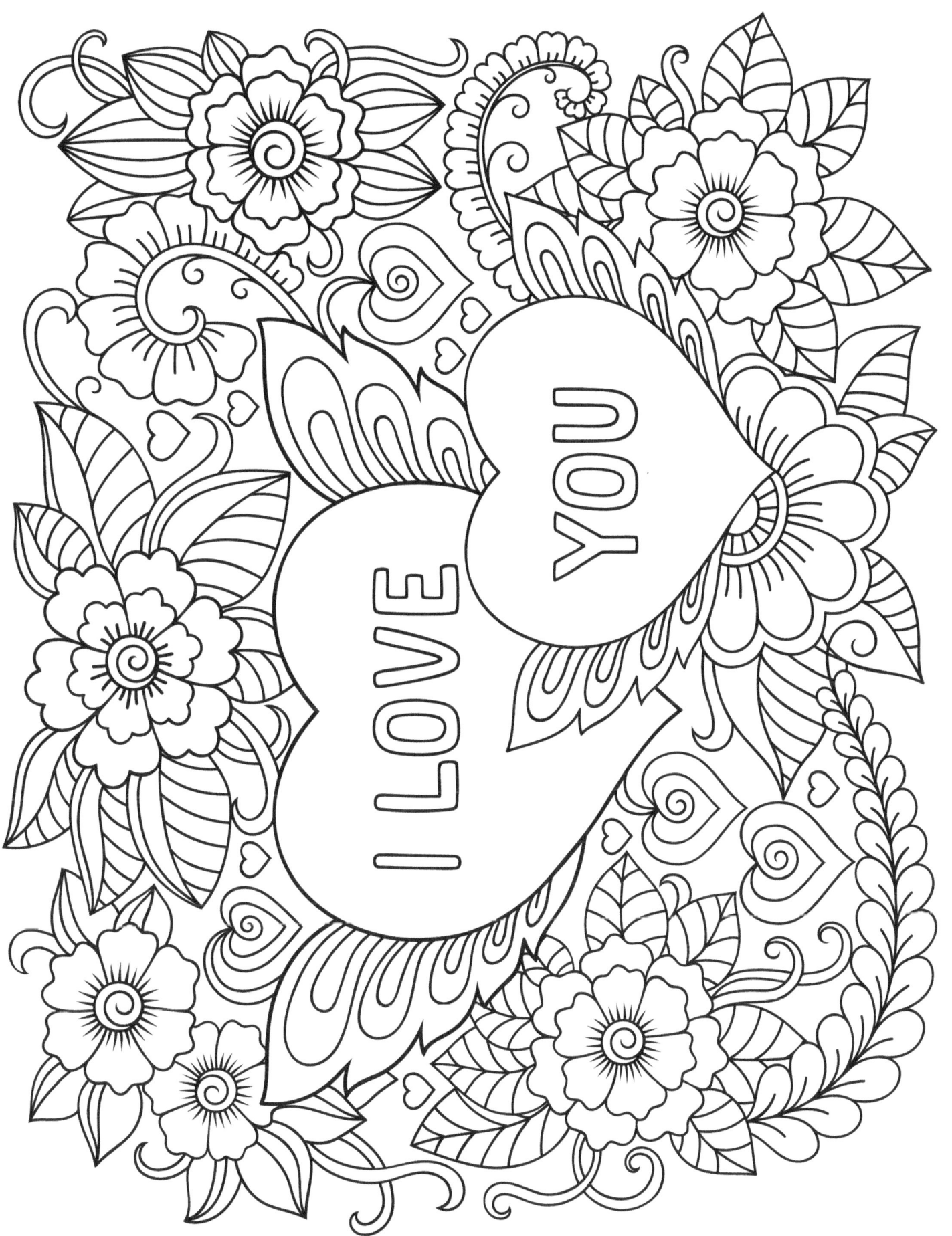

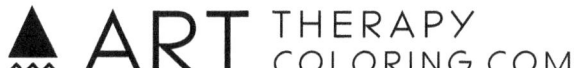

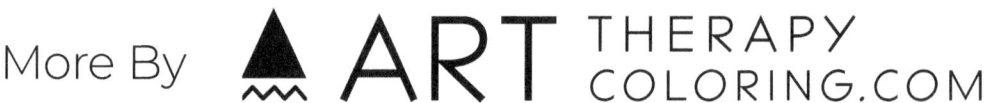
Best Selling Art Therapy Coloring Books

Coloring Books For Adults:

- Zombie Coloring Book: Black Background
- Butterfly Coloring Book For Adults: Black Background
- Tattoo Coloring Book: Black Background
- Coloring Books for Adults Relaxation: Native American Inspired Designs
- Fishing Coloring Book for Adults: Black Background

Coloring Books For Men:

- Coloring Book for Men: Anti-Stress Designs Vol 1
- Coloring Book For Men: Fishing Designs
- Coloring Book For Men: Tattoo Designs
- Coloring Books for Men: Hunting
- Coloring Book For Men: Biker Designs

Coloring Books For Seniors:

- Coloring Book For Seniors: Nature Designs Vol 1
- Coloring Book For Seniors: Anti-Stress Designs Vol 1
- Coloring Books for Seniors: Relaxing Designs
- Coloring Book For Seniors: Floral Designs Vol 1

Coloring Books For Teens and Tweens:

- Teen Coloring Books For Girls: Vol 1
- Tween Coloring Books For Girls: Cute Animals
- Coloring Books For Teens: Ocean Designs
- Coloring Books for Tweens: Fashion Girls
- Coloring Book for Teens: Anti-Stress Designs Vol 1

Coloring Books For Kids:

- Coloring Books For Girls: Cute Animals
- Horse Coloring Book For Girls
- Coloring Books For Boys: Sharks
- Unicorn Coloring Book for Girls
- Detailed Coloring Books For Kids

Art Therapy Coloring Books For Teens & Tweens

Coloring Books For Tweens

- Animal Coloring Book For Tweens: Zendoodle Designs
- Coloring Book For Tweens: Adorable Animals
- Coloring Book For Tweens: Detailed Animal Designs
- Coloring Book For Tweens: Zendoodle Stress Relief
- Coloring Book For Tweens: Stress Relieving Animals
- Tween Coloring Book: Stress Relieving Designs
- Tween Coloring Book: Wolves, Lions, Tigers
- Tween Coloring Book: Dragon Designs
- Tween Coloring Book: Zendoodle Animals
- Tween Coloring Book: Heart Designs
- Tween Coloring Book: Mermaid & Ocean Designs
- Tween Coloring Book: Ocean, Pirate, Skulls
- Tween Coloring Book: Anti-Stress Travel Designs
- Tween Coloring Book: Ocean Designs Vols. 1–3
- Tween Coloring Book: Stress Relief Vols. 1–2
- Tween Coloring Book: Cute Animal Designs
- Tween Coloring Book For Girls: Calming Stress Relief
- Tween Coloring Book For Girls: Anti-Stress Designs
- Tween Coloring Book For Girls: Meditative Stress Relief
- Coloring Book For Tween Boys: Skulls & More

Coloring Books for Teens:

- Teen Coloring Books For Girls: Swirls & Inspiration
- Teen Coloring Books For Girls: Stress Relieving Designs
- Coloring Books For Teens Relaxation: Dolphins & More
- Coloring Books For Teens Relaxation: Seahorses & More
- Coloring Books For Teens Relaxation: Sharks & More
- Coloring Books For Teens Relaxation: Wolves & More
- Teen Coloring Book: Inspirational Designs
- Teen Coloring Books: Animal Designs
- Coloring Books For Teen Boys: Detailed Designs: Black Background
- Teen Boys Coloring Book: Animal Designs
- Teen Coloring Books For Boys: Detailed Designs: Black Background
- Teen Coloring Books For Boys: Detailed Designs

Art Therapy Coloring Books

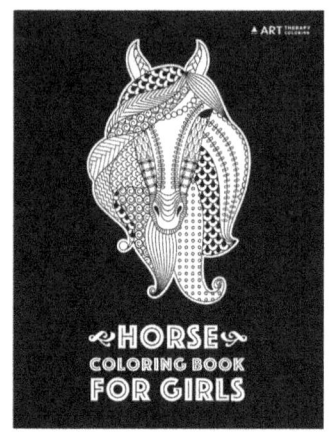

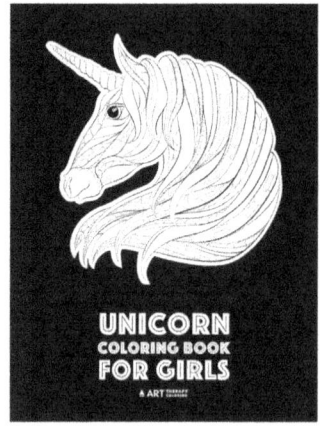

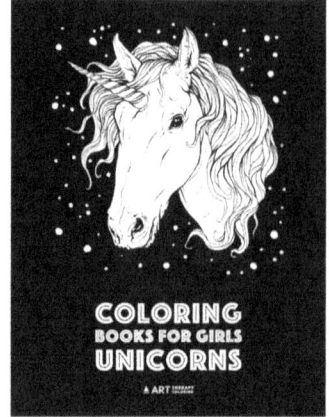

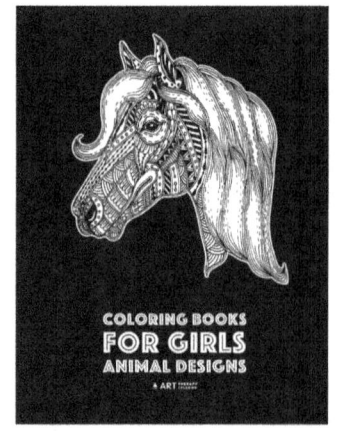

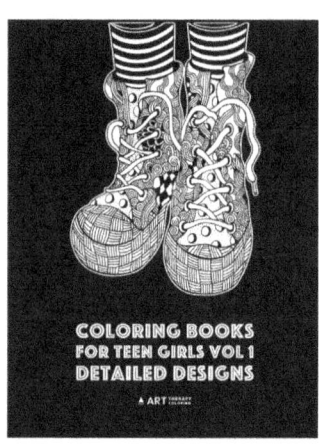

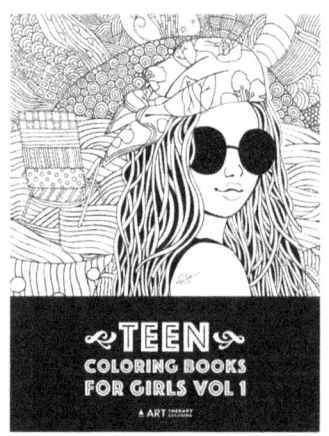

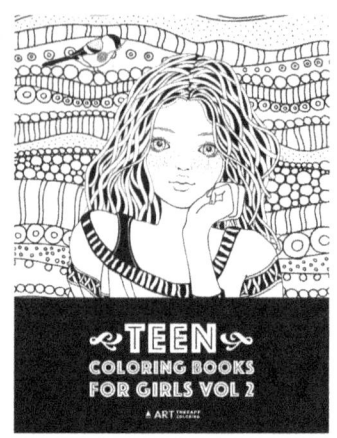

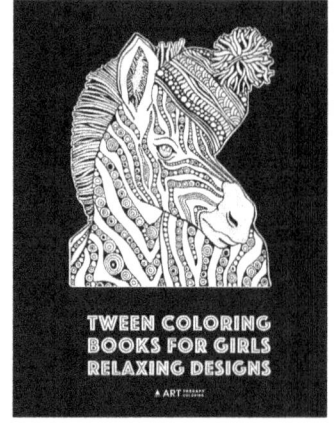

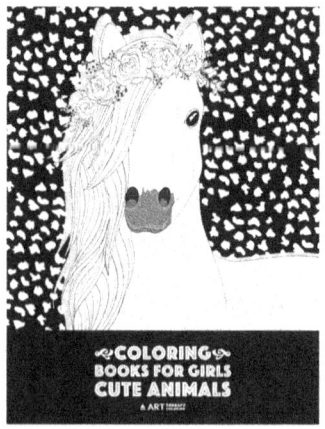

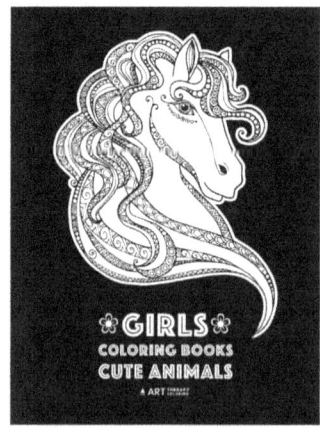

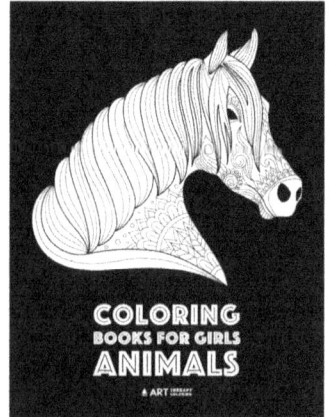

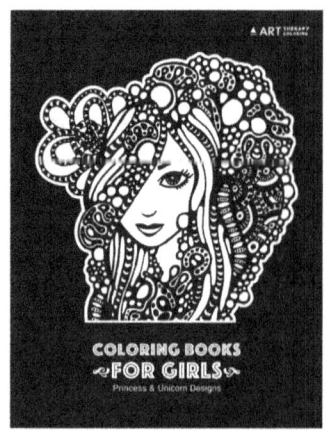

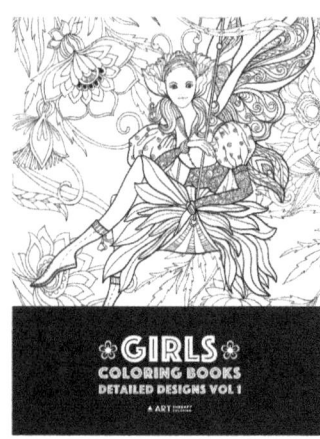

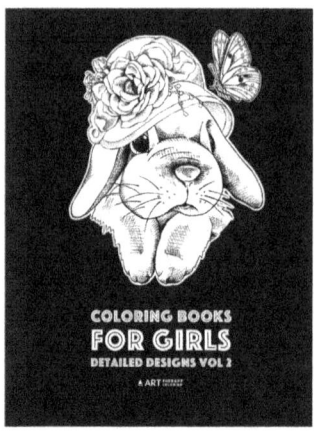

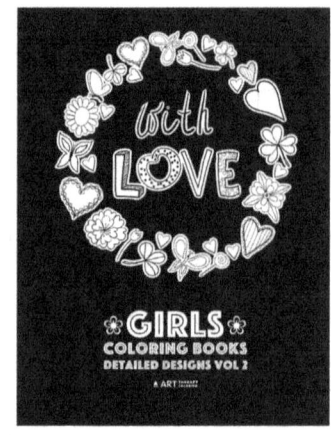

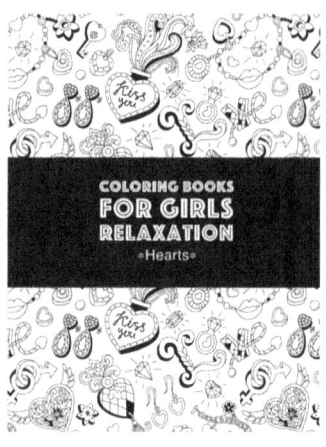

Art Therapy Coloring Books

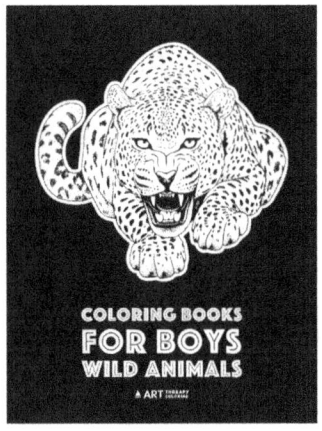

COLORING BOOKS
FOR BOYS
WILD ANIMALS

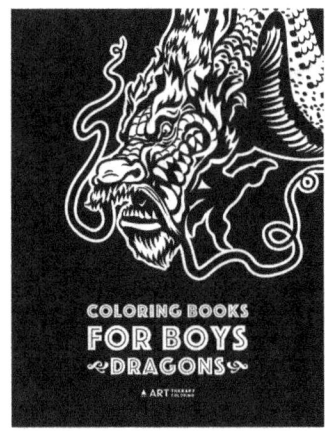

COLORING BOOKS
FOR BOYS
~ DRAGONS ~

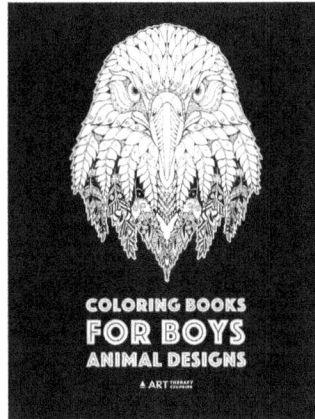

COLORING BOOKS
FOR BOYS
ANIMAL DESIGNS

COLORING BOOKS
FOR BOYS
OCEAN DESIGNS
Black Background

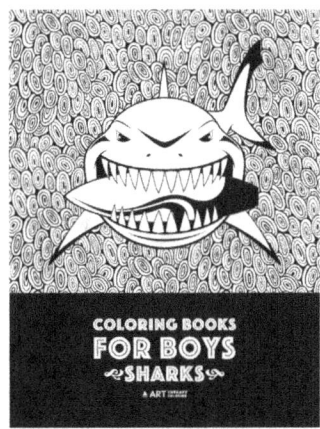

COLORING BOOKS
FOR BOYS
~ SHARKS ~

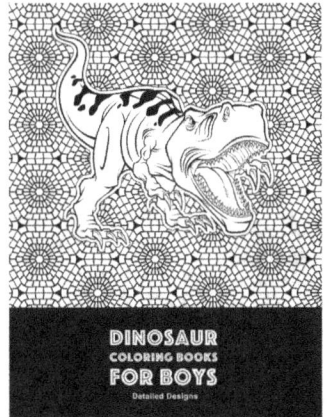

DINOSAUR
COLORING BOOKS
FOR BOYS
Detailed Designs

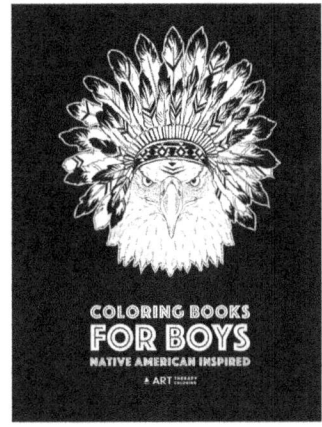

COLORING BOOKS
FOR BOYS
NATIVE AMERICAN INSPIRED

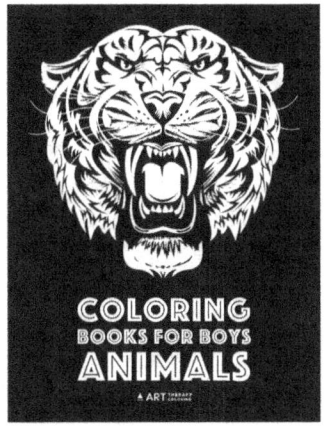

COLORING
BOOKS FOR BOYS
ANIMALS

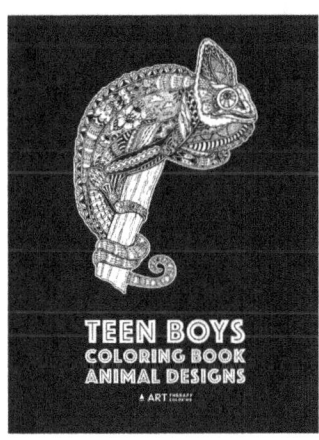

TEEN BOYS
COLORING BOOK
ANIMAL DESIGNS

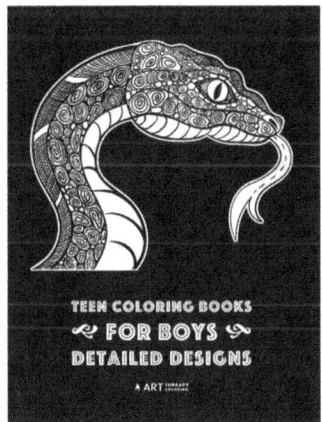

TEEN COLORING BOOKS
~ FOR BOYS ~
DETAILED DESIGNS

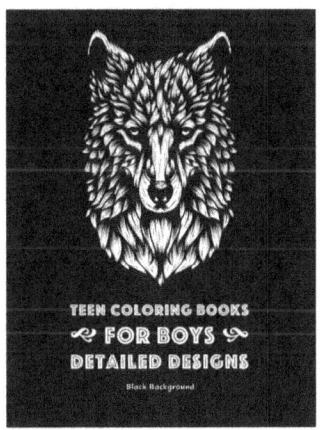

TEEN COLORING BOOKS
~ FOR BOYS ~
DETAILED DESIGNS
Black Background

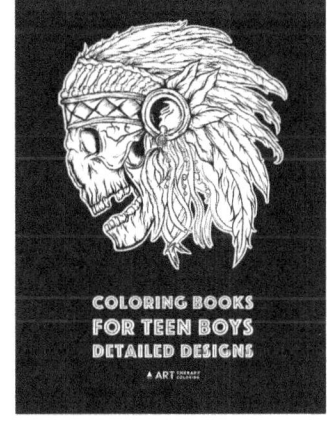

COLORING BOOKS
FOR TEEN BOYS
DETAILED DESIGNS

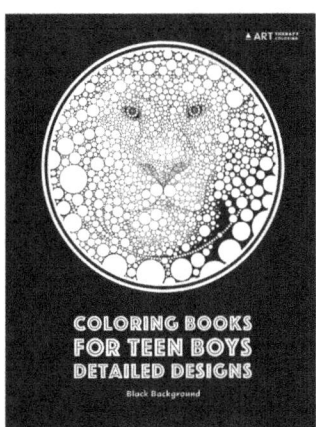

COLORING BOOKS
FOR TEEN BOYS
DETAILED DESIGNS
Black Background

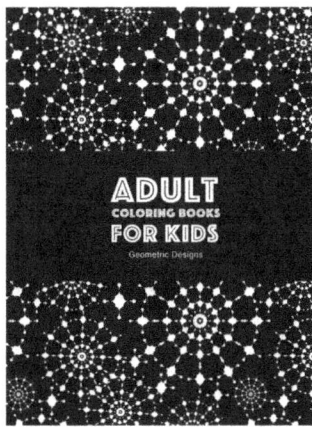

ADULT
COLORING BOOKS
FOR KIDS
Geometric Designs

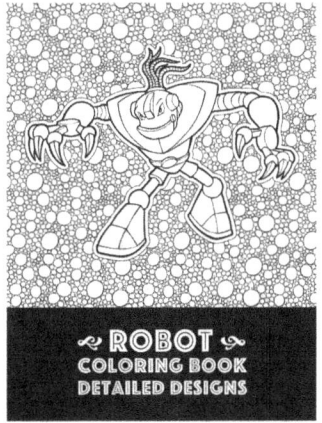

~ ROBOT ~
COLORING BOOK
DETAILED DESIGNS

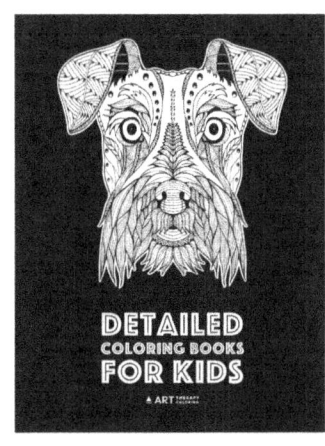

DETAILED
COLORING BOOKS
FOR KIDS

Art Therapy Coloring Books

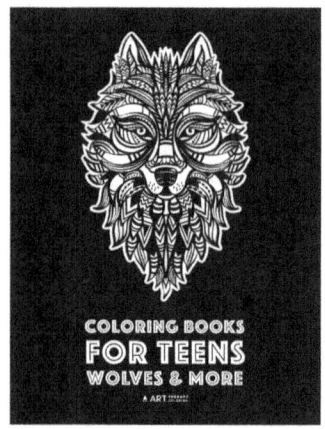

COLORING BOOKS FOR TEENS WOLVES & MORE

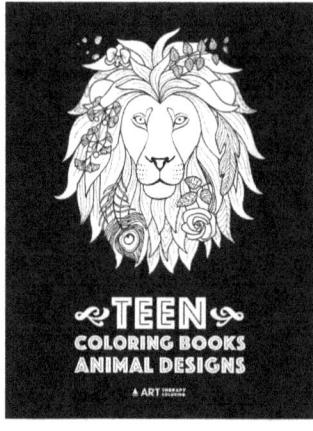

TEEN COLORING BOOKS ANIMAL DESIGNS

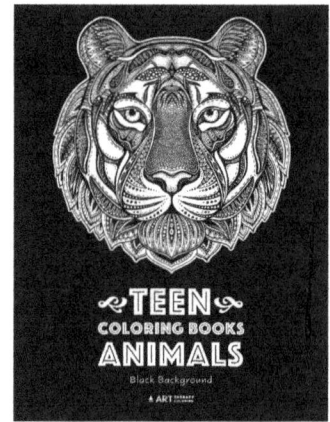

TEEN COLORING BOOKS ANIMALS Black Background

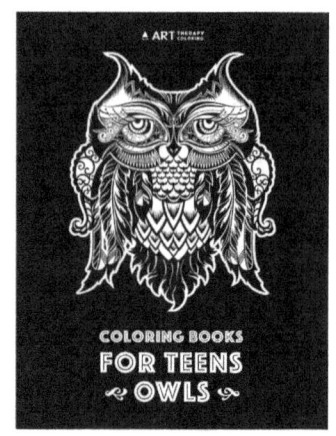

COLORING BOOKS FOR TEENS OWLS

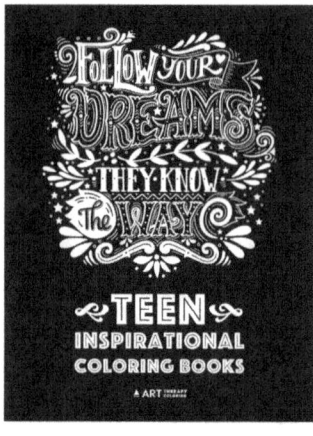

TEEN INSPIRATIONAL COLORING BOOKS

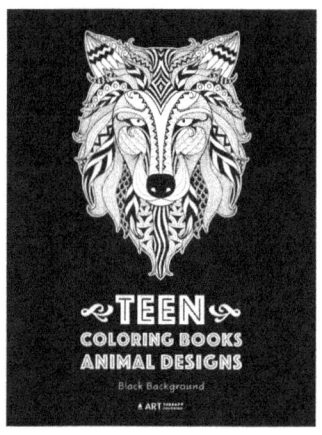

TEEN COLORING BOOKS ANIMAL DESIGNS Black Background

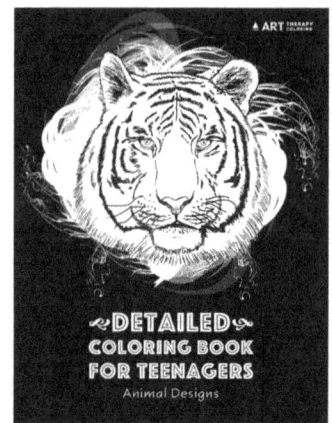

DETAILED COLORING BOOK FOR TEENAGERS Animal Designs

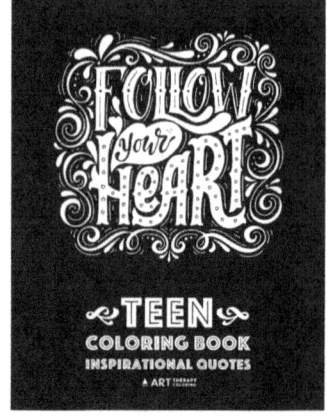

TEEN COLORING BOOK INSPIRATIONAL QUOTES

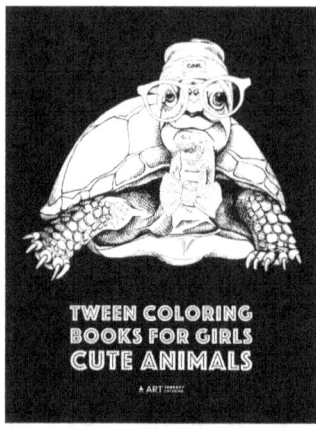

TWEEN COLORING BOOKS FOR GIRLS CUTE ANIMALS

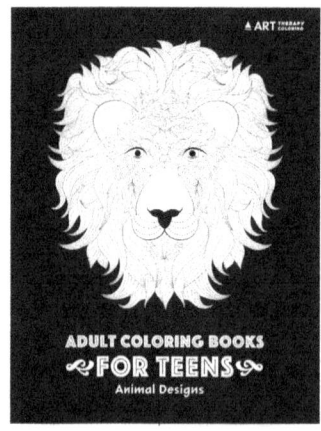

ADULT COLORING BOOKS FOR TEENS Animal Designs

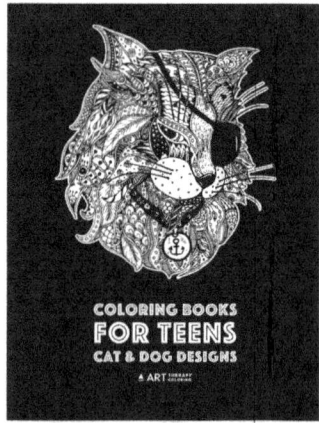

COLORING BOOKS FOR TEENS CAT & DOG DESIGNS

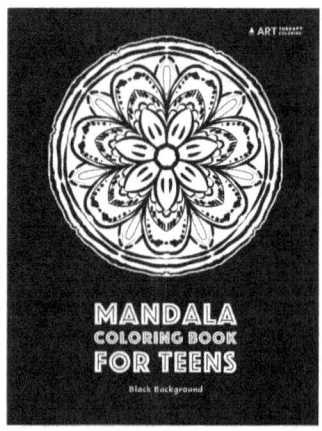

MANDALA COLORING BOOK FOR TEENS Black Background

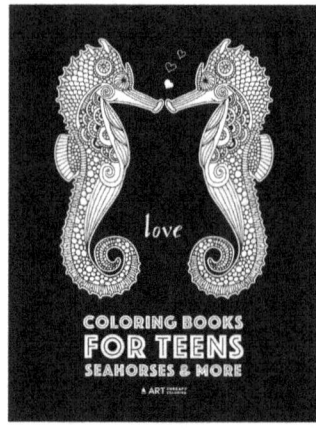

COLORING BOOKS FOR TEENS SEAHORSES & MORE

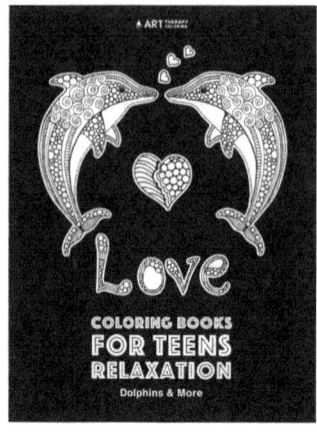

COLORING BOOKS FOR TEENS RELAXATION Dolphins & More

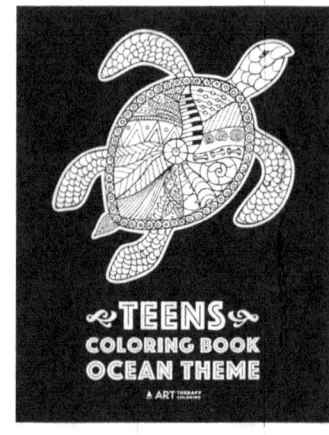

TEENS COLORING BOOK OCEAN THEME

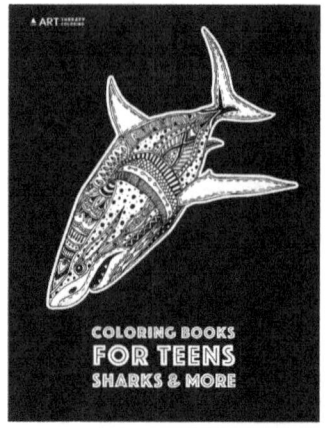

COLORING BOOKS FOR TEENS SHARKS & MORE

Art Therapy Coloring Books

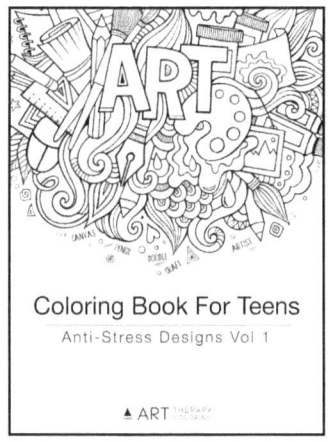

Coloring Book For Teens
Anti-Stress Designs Vol 1

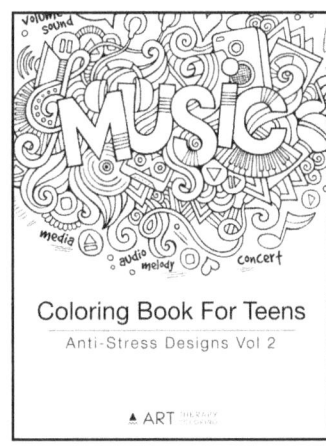

Coloring Book For Teens
Anti-Stress Designs Vol 2

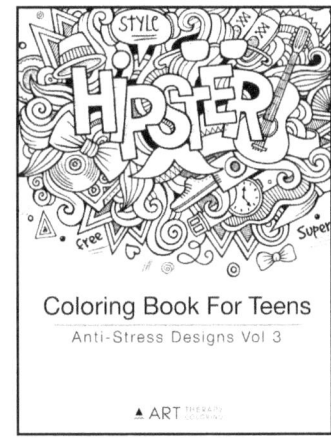

Coloring Book For Teens
Anti-Stress Designs Vol 3

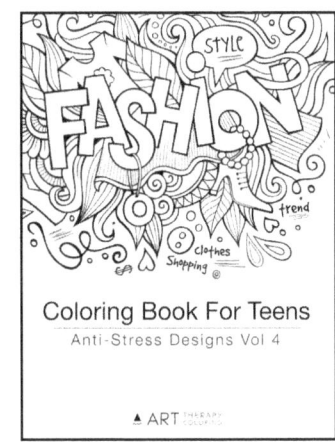

Coloring Book For Teens
Anti-Stress Designs Vol 4

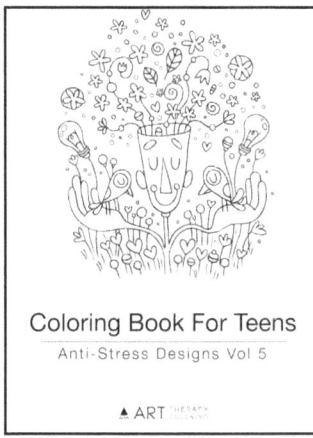

Coloring Book For Teens
Anti-Stress Designs Vol 5

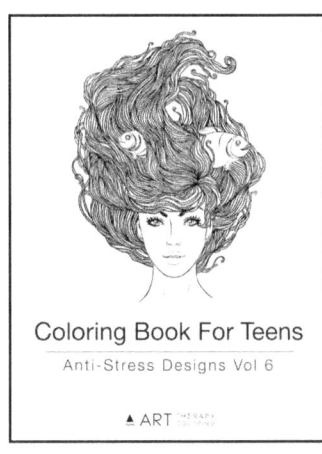

Coloring Book For Teens
Anti-Stress Designs Vol 6

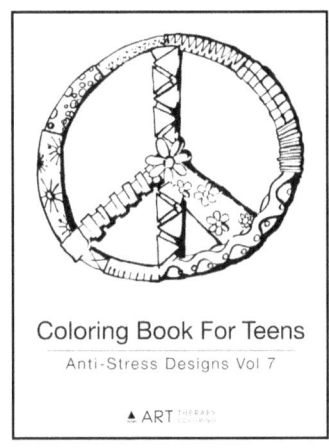

Coloring Book For Teens
Anti-Stress Designs Vol 7

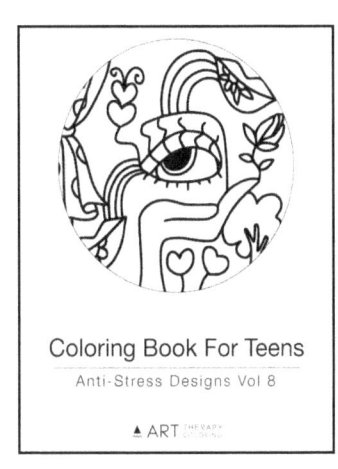

Coloring Book For Teens
Anti-Stress Designs Vol 8

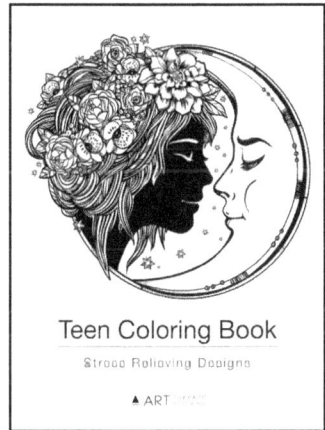

Teen Coloring Book
Stress Relieving Designs

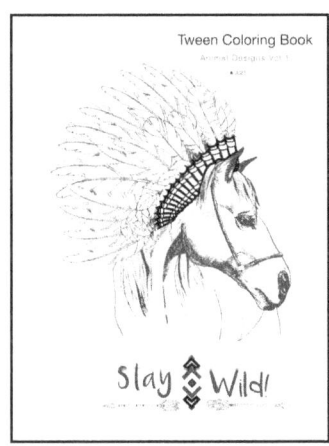

Tween Coloring Book

Slay Wild!

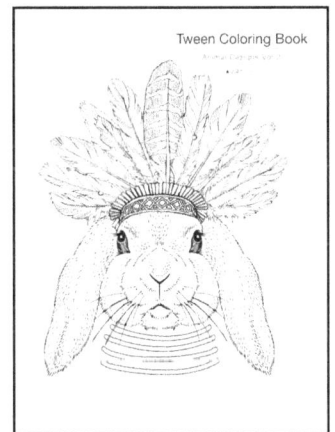

Tween Coloring Book

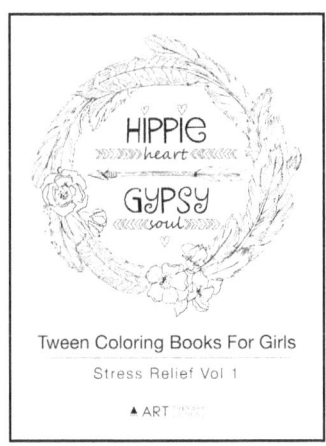

Tween Coloring Books For Girls
Stress Relief Vol 1

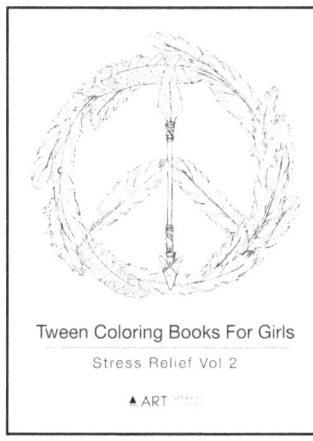

Tween Coloring Books For Girls
Stress Relief Vol 2

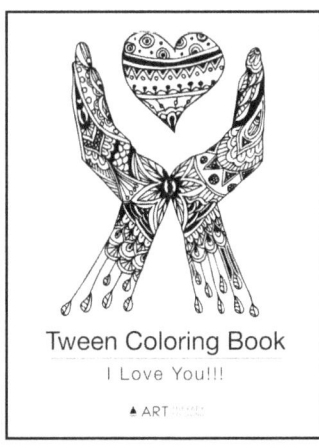

Tween Coloring Book
I Love You!!!

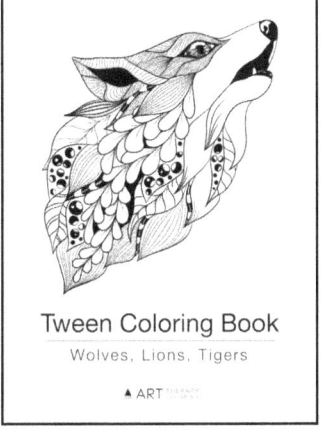

Tween Coloring Book
Wolves, Lions, Tigers

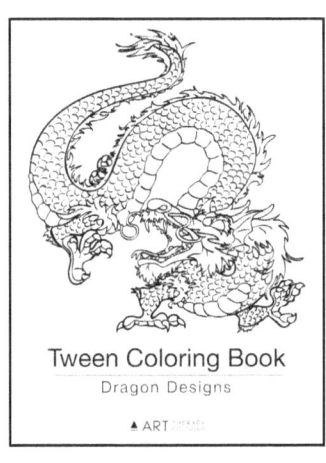

Tween Coloring Book
Dragon Designs

Tween Coloring Book For Girls
Stress Relief Designs

Published by:
Art Therapy Coloring
www.arttherapycoloring.com

Images Under License From Shutterstock